Soup's On!

Hot Recipes from Cool Chefs

Gail Hobbs & Bob Carter

Gem Guides Book Co.
315 Cloverleaf Drive, Suite F
Baldwin Park, CA 91706

Soup's On!
Hot Recipes from Cool Chefs

By Gail Hobbs & Bob Carter

Published by:
Gem Guides Book Co.
315 Cloverleaf Drive, Suite F
Baldwin Park, CA 91706
Tel: (626) 855-1611 Fax: (626) 855-1610

Copyright © 1997 by Gail Hobbs & Bob Carter
Cover Design by ¡JEFFE! Design & Prepress Solutions

Library of Congress Cataloging-in-Publication Data
Hobbs, Gail
        Soup's on: hot recipes from cool chefs /
        Gail Hobbs & Bob Carter.
            p.   cm.
        Includes index.
        ISBN 0-9642012-1-6
        1. Cookery, soup. I. Title.

96-094804
CIP

Printed in the United States of America

Every effort has been made by the authors to include only recipes not previously copyrighted. If a copyrighted recipe appears in this book, it is without the authors knowledge and is unintentional.

Acknowledgments

Our thanks to the incredible chefs, restaurants, bed and breakfast inns, hotels, and resorts, who generously shared their fabulous soup recipes and encouragement.

Soup's On! is dedicated to loving families, supportive friends, and soup lovers everywhere.

Contents

Introduction

UMMMMM........Soup. What can a humble pot of ordinary fixings do for you? On a chilly day a steaming bowl of richly seasoned soup has the power to warm the heart, soothe the soul, and fortify the weary. A cup of cool, spicy soup or chilled, sweet fruit purée can bring relief to a feverish brow on a sultry day. What more could you ask?

There's something special about soup. That's why we've gathered together more than 125 fabulous soup recipes from over 100 great chefs. We searched for savvy cooks, sensational restaurants, quaint B&Bs, traditional inns, historic hotels, glitzy resorts, and trendy places. We asked super chefs to share their incredible soup creations with us. The response was overwhelming. As a result, *Soup's On! Hot Recipes from Cool Chefs* is a collection of the best soup recipes from topnotch chefs in America, Canada, and the West Indies.

The chefs, eateries, and places to stay are fascinating, and we've included interesting tidbits about each. The descriptions are intended to highlight the unique flavor of each talented contributor. We hope to pique your interest and encourage you to seek out the people and places who appeal to you. We've made locating the address and the description easy for you by including a Contributors Directory on page 181. Where there's more than one recipe from a chef or destination, descriptive information is provided one time only.

Throughout the book, you'll see two symbols: a soup pot and chef's hat. They are used to designate the soup recipe and the corresponding contributor.

Although some of the soup recipes have been adapted slightly for consistency in format, we've allowed each contributor's personality to shine through. Whenever possible, we've included the chef's personal comments about his or her recipe.

If you stumble upon a favorite soup during your travels, we'd love to hear from you. Send us the name and address of the chef or restaurant. We'll contact them and consider adding your discovery to the next edition of our *Soup's On!* cookbook.

Now it's time to get out the fixings, brew-up a sensational soup, and travel with us on a refreshing culinary journey.

Bon Appétit!

Gail Hobbs & Bob Carter

Soup
Basics

Tips for Sensational Soup

Soup can be served any way you like it: hot or cold, smooth or creamy, thick or chunky, mild or spicy. You can savor a cup of soup before a formal meal or indulge in a hearty bowlful for a complete meal. However you satisfy your passion for soup, the following tips and hints will help you individualize it to suit your personal taste.

To thicken soup: Briskly simmer the soup uncovered to reduce liquid volume, add a roux (cooked butter or oil and flour mixture), or purée some of the soup's ingredients.

Seasonings: Aside from following the soup recipe directions, the kind and amount of herbs and spices used in cooking is a matter of personal preference. For example, if a recipe calls for cayenne pepper and you love hot, spicy food, just add a little extra.

Fresh herbs are the most flavorful: Even if you don't have a garden, you can grow the herbs you use most often on the windowsill. Parsley, basil, chives, dill, mint, oregano, thyme, and sage are a few of the common herbs that grow well in pots.

To reduce the calories in a soup: Cut back a little on the amount of fat called for in the recipe and choose a soup (like vegetable) where the main ingredients are naturally low in calories. Imitate a creamy consistency by puréeing some of the vegetables instead of adding cream.

For the best flavored soup: Soup benefits greatly if allowed to sit in the refrigerator overnight so the flavors can develop.

Garnishing soup: Garnishing a bowl of soup will help make an attractive presentation. To garnish successfully, choose an ingredient from the soup or a contrasting, complementary ingredient. A small amount of finely diced or julienne vegetables, meat, or poultry, a single shellfish, or minced herbs make good garnishes. Try sour cream, grated cheeses, popcorn, croutons, slivered or chopped nuts, citrus wedges or curls, and seasonings. Experiment, the possibilities are endless.

Serving containers: Match the serving container with the soup you're serving. Dish up a light, delicate appetizer soup in a small cup and a hearty main-course soup in a good-sized bowl. A chilled fruit purée looks appetizing in a clear parfait cup. For a festive presentation use the shell of one of the soup's main ingredients as a bowl. For example, a large pumpkin or squash shell holds a batch of soup to be taken to the table and served family-style. A small fruit or vegetable like an orange or a small squash shell holds individual servings of soup.

Preparing the bowl: Cut a lid off the top and shave just enough off the bottom to get a level surface without cutting all the way through (or the soup will leak out). Then, scoop out the pulp. To stabilize the homemade bowl, so it won't tip over, set it on a plate or in a larger bowl with a nest of shredded lettuce or parsley. Bread rounds also make great, edible serving bowls. Prepare them the same as you would a fruit or vegetable bowl.

Accompaniments: A warm loaf of fresh bread goes perfectly with homemade soup. Try breadsticks, plain or savory crackers, and garlic or herb toast, too.

Useful Cooking Terms

Bisque: A thick, rich cream soup usually made with shellfish or puréed vegetables.

Boil: To cook liquid rapidly so bubbles rise constantly to the surface and break.

Bouillon: A clear, usually seasoned, broth made by straining water in which meat, poultry, or vegetables has been cooked. May be made by dissolving a bouillon cube or granules in boiling water.

Bouillon cube: A small cube of dehydrated beef, chicken, or vegetable stock.

Bouquet garni: A bundle of several herbs, usually parsley, thyme, and bay leaves, tied into a cheesecloth used to flavor soups and stews. The sachet can be removed when desired.

Broth: (Stock) A liquid in which meat, poultry, fish, or vegetables (or a combination) has been cooked.

Chiffonade: A mixture of finely cut vegetables or herbs for use in soups and salads.

Concasse: Peeled, seeded, and coarsely chopped tomatoes.

Crème fraîche: What the French call their thick, tart, fresh cream.

Chop: To cut into small pieces.

Cube: To cut into square-shaped pieces about 1/2-inch.

Dice: To cut into small cubes of uniform size about 1/4-inch.

Garnish: To decorate food or a plate with small pieces of food to provide color or texture.

Julienne: Long, thin strips of meats, vegetables, or other foods.

Mince: To cut into very small pieces about 1/8-inch.

Potage: Soup.

Purée: To convert food into a thick, smooth paste by pressing through a food mill or whirling in a blender or food processor.

Sauté: To cook in a small amount of hot fat.

Simmer: To cook in liquid just below the boiling point (over low heat) so bubbles form at a slow rate and break before reaching the surface.

Skim: To remove fat or foam from the surface of a liquid using a spoon or bulb baster.

Stock: (Broth) The liquor or broth prepared by boiling meat, poultry, fish, vegetables and used as a foundation for soups and stews.

Common Substitutions

It's always best to use the exact ingredients listed in a recipe. However, sometimes you're in the middle of cooking and discover you don't have a precise ingredient on hand. In a pinch, you can use the alternative ingredients listed below. It's best not to use more than one or two substitutions in each recipe.

When the recipe call for:	You can substitute:
1 cup whole milk	1 cup nonfat milk plus 2 tablespoons butter or margarine
1 cup nonfat or skim milk	1/3 cup instant nonfat dry milk plus enough water to make 1 cup
1 cup buttermilk	1 cup plain yogurt or 1 tablespoon lemon juice or vinegar plus enough milk to make 1 cup. Let stand for 5 minutes before using
1 cup cream or half-and-half	3/4 cup milk plus 1/3 cup butter or margarine, melted and cooled
1 cup butter or margarine	7/8 cup vegetable oil
1 cup sour cream	1 cup plain yogurt
Crème fraîche	1 cup heavy cream plus 1 tablespoon buttermilk or 1/4 cup sour cream. Heat just until barely warm to the touch and let sit at room temperature, covered with cheesecloth, for 6 to 8 hours.
Juice of 1 lemon	3 tablespoons bottled lemon juice

1 cup broth	1 bouillon cube dissolved in 1 cup boiling water
16 ounces canned tomatoes	2-1/2 cups peeled, chopped fresh tomatoes simmered for 10 minutes
1 teaspoon dry mustard	1 tablespoon prepared mustard
1 clove garlic	1 teaspoon minced fresh garlic or 1/8 teaspoon garlic powder
1 teaspoon grated fresh ginger	1/2 teaspoon ground ginger
1 tablespoon fresh herbs	1 to 2 teaspoons dried herbs

Basic Measurements

3 teaspoons = 1 tablespoon
2 tablespoons = 1 fluid ounce
2 tablespoons = 1/8 cup
4 tablespoons = 1/4 cup
1/2 cup = 4 fluid ounces
1 cup = 8 fluid ounces
2 cups = 16 fluid ounces = 1 pint
4 cups = 2 pints = 1 quart
1 quart = 1 liter +1.8 ounces
8 cups = 2 quarts = 1/2 gallon
16 cups = 4 quarts = 1 gallon

Soup Seasonings

One of the keys to flavoring soups is knowing how to use herbs and spices. This list describes many of the seasonings used in *Soup's On!* recipes.

Herbs are flowering plants whose stem grows above ground and do not become woody. Usually the leaves, and sometimes the seeds, are used for flavoring food. Whenever possible, use fresh herbs for cooking. They can be grown in small gardens and windowsill pots, or purchased. Fresh herbs can be dried and stored in airtight glass jars in a cool, dark place.

Spices are generally the roots, bark, pods, berries, or seeds of aromatic plants used to season food. Many are grown in the tropics. Whole spices keep their pungency longer than ground. Store in airtight, glass jars in a cool, dark place.

Bay leaves. Whole leaves are used in soups. Should be removed before serving.

Basil. Spicy, sweet flavor. Use with tomato-based soups, eggplant, and spinach.

Caraway seeds. Use with cabbage, sauerkraut, hearty meats.

Cardamom. Whole or ground. Member of the ginger family. Ingredient in curry powder.

Chervil. Parsley-like leaves. Use with fish and eggs.

Chili Pepper. A type of capsicum (a common garden pepper, occurring in many varieties ranging from mild to hot). Generally available whole, fresh, dried, flakes, crushed, and ground (**cayenne pepper**, for example). Use in spicy foods. *May be spelled several ways. *Soup's On!* uses chili and chilies, except when quoting a chef.

Chives. Thin tubular leaves, mild onion-like flavor. Use with eggs, cheese, white fish, potatoes, and as a garnish.

Cilantro. Fresh leaves have a peppery flavor. Use in Mexican and Chinese dishes. Seeds are called **coriander** and are an ingredient in curry powder.

Cinnamon. Sticks of rolled bark or ground. Use in baking cookies and cakes, fruit dishes, and sweet vegetables.

Cumin. Whole or ground. A main curry ingredient. Use in Mexican, Middle Eastern, and Indian dishes.

Curry powder. A blend of up to 12 spices including cumin, coriander, turmeric, ginger, pepper, mace, cardamom, and cloves. Golden in color. Use in salad dressings and cheese dishes, and with eggs.

Dill. Chopped leaves used with seafood and eggs, in sauces, and as a garnish.

Fennel. Licorice-like flavor. Thick stalks are eaten raw or cooked like celery. Widely used in Italian cooking. Seeds are used in baked goods.

Fine herbes. An herb blend, usually a combination of parsley, chervil, tarragon, and chives. Use with vegetables, eggs, and fish.

Garlic. A member of the onion family available whole fresh, crushed, ground, and with salt. Strong-flavored cloves used as a seasoning, a condiment, and a vegetable.

Ginger. Hot, sweet taste. Available whole, crystallized, and ground. Use with chicken, mild white fish, baked goods, curries, and in Asian dishes.

Italian seasoning. A blend of herbs, usually oregano, basil, marjoram, and thyme. Use in Italian dishes and salad dressings; with meats and poultry.

Marjoram. Use leaves in tomato-based and vegetable soups, and with lamb, eggs, eggplant, and summer squash.

Mint. Strong, sweet flavor and aroma with a cool aftertaste. Many varieties. Use in chilled fruit soups, drinks, and with lamb and vegetables.

Nutmeg. Sweet flavor and aroma. Use same as cinnamon in baked goods and with sweet vegetables.

Oregano. Leaves or ground. Use in Italian- and Mexican-style dishes; tomato-based and vegetable soups; and pasta dishes.

Parsley. Fresh, mildly-flavored leaves widely used with many foods and as a garnish.

Rosemary. Needlelike leaves used in stuffings, meat, poultry, and cheese dishes.

Saffron. Most expensive spice. Strands or ground. Imparts an orange color to Indian, Middle Eastern, South American, and Mediterranean dishes. Use with rice, poultry, and seafood.

Sage. Leaves or ground for pork, poultry, stuffings, mushrooms, and onions.

Tarragon. Use leaves with eggs, seafood, and poultry.

Thyme. Pungent flavor. Leaves or ground. Add to chowders, tomato sauces, poultry, and vegetables.

Turmeric. Available ground. Bright yellow color. Use in curry powder, pickles, pork, fish, and chicken.

Homemade Stock

Stock is one of the most important flavor ingredients in soup. That's why great soup cooks make their own stock. It's easy to do. In fresh water, cook vegetables, sometimes adding meat, poultry, or fish, with herbs and seasonings. Soup can be prepared using one of four basic stock recipes: vegetable, meat, chicken, or fish. Use the following suggestions, and the stock recipes in this chapter, and you're on your way to making a fabulous homemade stock.

To make an aromatic, flavorful stock, always begin with the freshest and finest ingredients available.

Vegetables should be fresh (or frozen, if you must,) crisp, blemish free, and washed with cold water. For intense flavor, thoroughly sauté a variety of full-bodied vegetables in a little hot oil or butter. Heating releases the sweetness of onions and garlic and brings out the best in carrots and celery.

Meats, poultry, and seafood should be fresh or fresh-frozen and free from strong odors.

Use fresh herbs if available. If not, use dried herbs. Herbs should be less than one year old and stored in airtight containers to retain their flavor. As a general rule, substitute 1/3 the amount of dried for fresh. 1 teaspoon dried equals 1 tablespoon fresh.

Good-tasting water is essential for a good-tasting stock. If you drink your tap water, you can cook with it. If you buy bottled water then use it for cooking.

Although homemade stocks are preferred by many chefs, don't allow the lack of one stop you from making homemade soup. Canned beef, chicken, and vegetable broths are readily available in grocery stores along with bouillon cubes and granules. You'll also find a variety of concentrated stock bases such as beef, chicken, and clam. Commercially prepared stocks usually contain a high amount of sodium. Unless you choose to use a low-sodium stock, don't add any salt to the soup until it's finished cooking *and* you've tasted it. If you accidentally end up with too much salt in your soup, add a couple of large slices of raw potato and simmer for 20 minutes. The potato absorbs the excess salt,

Homemade Stocks

Vegetable Stock

A flavorful vegetable stock is the most versatile of all the stocks. It can be used in a pinch in place of any other stock. Although the flavor of the soup will vary somewhat, it's always preferable to using plain water. Vegetarians depend on vegetable stock instead of one made with meat. The basic rule for making homemade is to use at least one cup of vegetables or cleaned scraps to each cup of cold water. The vegetables in this basic recipe will produce a nice fragrant stock. Be cautious about using strong flavored vegetables like asparagus, broccoli, and cauliflower because they will overpower the stock.

Makes approximately 12 cups.

2 tablespoons butter or oil
4 to 6 cups mixed chopped
** vegetables such as onions,**
** carrots, celery, potatoes,**
** mushrooms, garlic &**
** tomatoes**

1/2 cup chopped fresh parsley
1/4 cup chopped fresh basil
3 or 4 bay leaves
1 teaspoon whole peppercorns
1 gallon cold water

Heat butter or oil in a stockpot. Add chopped vegetables and sauté for 10 minutes until lightly browned and fragrant. Add herbs, seasonings, and cold water. Bring to a boil. Reduce heat and gently simmer, partially covered, for approximately 2 hours. Cool slightly, strain, and use immediately. May be stored in the refrigerator for several days or frozen for up to three months.

Leftover Vegetable Stock: Save all cleaned vegetable peels and trimmings to use in place of whole vegetables. Save liquid from canned, boiled, or steamed vegetables. Keep a plastic container with a tight-fitting lid in the freezer. Add leftover broth as well.

Rich Vegetable Stock: For a richer, more flavorful stock, follow directions for basic stock except raise heat and simmer briskly, uncovered, to reduce liquid volume. Add seasonings as desired.

Dry Vegetable Broth/Mix: Fresh homemade vegetable stock is ideal. If you don't have any, and you're short on time, make a basic mix out of herbs and spices on hand. Mix the following together: 1 tablespoon *each* onion powder and garlic powder, 2 tablespoons dried parsley, 1/2 teaspoon *each* dried thyme, basil, oregano, celery powder, dill, and black pepper. Makes about 18 servings of 1 teaspoon each. Use 1 serving per cup of water. Store the rest in a jar with a tight-fitting lid.

Meat Stock

Some of the soup recipes in Soup's On! *call for a meat stock. You can use the following recipe and add the meat used in the soup you're making.*

Makes approximately 12 cups.

4 to 5 pounds lean, meaty beef, veal, lamb, ham, or game bones, broken or cut in pieces

2 *each* onions, carrots, & celery, chopped

1 *each* turnip & tomato, chopped

1 whole head garlic, smashed or 2 or 3 tablespoons minced

1 cup chopped parsley

2 tablespoons *each* thyme & oregano

3 or 4 bay leaves

1/2 to 1 teaspoon whole peppercorns

Water to cover, approximately 1 gallon

Roast meaty bones, onions, carrots, celery, turnip, tomato, and garlic in a large pan in a 450-degree oven for 45 minutes to 1 hour. Turning occasionally until well browned. Place meaty bones, vegetables, and flavorful scrappings from bottom of roasting pan into a large stockpot. Add seasonings and water to cover. Bring to a boil. Reduce heat and simmer, partially covered, for approximately 4 or 5 hours, stirring occasionally. Keep bones covered with water and skim foam as necessary. When stock is done, cool slightly, and strain. Refrigerate until chilled and remove fat from surface.

Rich, Concentrated Stock: For a more deeply flavored stock, raise heat and simmer briskly, uncovered, to reduce liquid volume. Add flavor by adding seasonings and a cup or two of hearty red wine, if desired.

White Meat Stock: Omit browning meaty bones or vegetables in oven. Instead add directly to stockpot with rest of ingredients and cook as directed.

Chicken Stock

This basic chicken stock recipe makes a mild, lean, unsalted broth.
Makes about 8 cups.

2 tablespoons vegetable oil
1 medium onion, chopped
1 large carrot, chopped
1/2 cup chopped celery and
  leafy tops
3 or 4 cloves garlic, smashed

3 to 4 pound whole chicken,
  cut up or meaty chicken parts
12 cups cold water
3 or 4 sprigs fresh parsley
10 or 12 whole peppercorns

Heat oil in a large stockpot. Add vegetables and sauté over high heat for 5 to 10 minutes or until lightly browned. Add chicken pieces, cold water, parsley, and peppercorns. Bring to a boil, then lower heat and gently simmer, partially covered, for approximately 2 hours. Skim foam off the top as it rises.

When stock is done, remove from heat and allow to cool slightly. Strain broth and refrigerate several hours or overnight. Remove congealed fat layer. Store in the refrigerator for up to a week or freeze for several months. The cooked chicken meat may be used for sandwiches, casseroles, or soup. To make chicken stock for same-day use, remove the skin and all visible fat from chicken and cook as directed. Strain broth and use as desired.

Leftover Stock: Save clean vegetable trimmings and peelings in a plastic bag in the freezer and use instead of whole vegetables. A chicken carcass or leftover bones with a little meat left on may be used instead of chicken pieces to make the stock.

Rich, Dark Stock: Roast chicken (or bones) with vegetables in a 450-degree oven for 30 to 45 minutes until well browned. Then, proceed preparing stock as directed.

Highly Flavored Stock: Increase heat to a brisk simmer and cook until liquid is reduced. Season as desired.

Homemade Stocks

Fish Stock

Soup recipes that call for fish stock will benefit greatly from a fresh, mild, homemade stock. If you don't need a gallon, halve the recipe.

Makes approximately 1 gallon.

2 tablespoons butter or oil
1 large onion, chopped
1/2 cup chopped mushrooms
2 or 3 cloves garlic, smashed or
   1 tablespoon minced
1 small lemon, quartered
1/2 cup chopped fresh parsley

1/2 teaspoon whole peppercorns
3 or 4 pounds mild, white fish
   bones and trimmings
1 gallon cold water
2 cups dry white wine

Heat butter or oil in a stockpot. Add onion, mushrooms, and garlic. Sauté for 5 or 6 minutes until lightly browned. Add lemon, parsley, peppercorns, fish trimmings, cold water, and wine. Bring to a boil, then lower heat and simmer gently, uncovered, for about 1 hour, skimming foam as necessary. Allow to cool slightly, strain, and use as desired. Refrigerate for 2 to 3 days, or freeze for several months.

Fish Fumet: Another name for a highly seasoned fish stock. Add a chopped carrot, chopped celery stalk, and a couple of bay leaves to the basic fish stock. Raise the heat and simmer briskly, uncovered, to reduce liquid volume. May also be used to poach fish.

Shrimp Stock: In his cookbook, *From the Earth to the Table*, Chef John Ash suggests saving shrimp shells in a bag in the freezer and adding a splash or two of dry white wine to a basic chicken stock to make a good shellfish or shrimp stock. He also strongly favors shrimp stock over store-bought bottled clam juice.

Crab Stock: Chandler's Crabhouse sent this recipe for the stock used in their Whiskeyed Crab Soup. Heat 2 tablespoons olive oil in a heavy stockpot. Add shells from 1 Dungeness crab, 1/4 cup *each* chopped carrot and celery, and 1/2 cup chopped onion. Brown lightly. Add 1/4 cup brandy or cognac and ignite. When flames have expired, add 4 cups cold water, 4 tablespoons tomato paste, 2 cloves garlic, crushed with skin on, 1 bay leaf, and 1 teaspoon dried tarragon. Bring stock to a low simmer for 2 to 3 hours, occasionally skimming the surface as needed. Cool slightly, strain through a fine sieve, and refrigerate until ready to use.

Homemade Stocks

Vegetable Soups

☐ *Garfield's Broccoli and Almond Soup*

Maxwell's is a casual, informal restaurant that boasts of having something for everyone. Broccoli and Almond Soup is homemade and loved by many loyal customers.

Yields 12 bowls.

1 gallon water
4 chicken bouillon cubes
2 pounds fresh broccoli,
  cut up
1 medium carrot, grated
2 teaspoons garlic powder
1/2 cup butter

1/2 cup margarine
1 cup flour
1/2 cup sherry
Salt & pepper to taste
1 cup blanched almonds
1 tablespoon monosodium
  glutamate

In a large pan, bring water to a boil and dissolve bouillon cubes. Add broccoli, carrot, and garlic. Cook for about 30 to 45 minutes. In a separate deep pan, melt butter and margarine. Add flour and cook to make a roux. Stir into broccoli mixture and cook until slightly thickened. Add sherry, salt, and pepper. Stir almonds and monosodium glutamate into soup.

☘ Maxwell's Restaurant & Lounge
Vicksburg, Mississippi

Located a short half mile from Vicksburg National Military Park and Vicksburg Civil War Museum, Maxwell's Restaurant & Lounge specializes in a variety of satisfying menu items.

Customer favorites include seafood gumbo, oysters galore, stuffed mushrooms, prime rib of beef au jus, steak and lobster, crab-stuffed flounder, pork chops with pineapple sauce, and veal Oscar. A special menu serves up tasty items for youngsters: hamburgers, chicken fingers, catfish filets, and spaghetti.

☐ *Max's Cabbage Soup*

Chef Max fortifies Toronto travelers with his wholesome Cabbage Soup.

Makes approximately 8 servings.

2 tablespoons butter	4 whole cloves
1 small cabbage, diced	3 whole bay leaves
1 cup chopped onion	Salt & pepper to taste
8 cups chicken stock	Fresh chopped parsley for
6 whole black peppercorns	garnish

In a Dutch oven or large saucepan, melt butter. Then sauté cabbage and onions, stirring often over medium heat until onions are transparent and lightly golden. Add stock, peppercorns, cloves, and bay leaves. Bring to a boil, reduce heat, and simmer for 1 hour.

Season to taste with salt and pepper. Remove whole spices and bay leaves. Ladle into bowls. Sprinkle with parsley and serve.

♧ Holiday Inn Toronto Airport
Toronto, Canada

Conveniently located, the Holiday Inn Toronto Airport provides close-in accommodations, restaurants, and convention and banquet facilities to travelers. The 444-room hotel is 20 minutes away from shopping centers, downtown Toronto, Black Creek Pioneer Village, Wild Water Kingdom, and Canada's Wonderland.

Several dining choices include the Metro Bar & Grill and the Roof Garden, located on the 12th floor overlooking the airport. Snookers Recreation club offers oak billiard tables, darts, board games, library, and bar.

⬜ *Carrot & Fresh Ginger Cream Soup*

Charming, alfresco Nona's Courtyard Café specializes in dishes that represent a fusion of California and Northern Italian cuisines.

Makes approximately 10 cups.

3 red onions, diced
1-1/2 cups butter
3 inches fresh ginger, smashed
3 pounds carrots, peeled & diced
1/2 teaspoon salt
5 turns black pepper mill

8 cups water or stock
1/4 cup honey
Juice of 1/2 a lemon
1 cup heavy cream
Paprika for garnish
Shredded carrot for garnish

Simmer onions with butter until translucent. Add smashed ginger, diced carrots, salt, and freshly ground black pepper. Pour in water or stock and simmer for 45 minutes.

Purée soup. Stir in honey, juice from 1/2 of a lemon, and heavy cream. Adjust salt to taste. Garnish individual serving bowls with a sprinkle of paprika and shredded carrot.

۞ Nona's Courtyard Café
Ventura, California

Nona's Courtyard Café, tucked away in downtown Ventura, offers intimate surroundings and exceptional food. The restaurant is located in the vine-covered courtyard of the historic Bella Maggiore Inn. It's an enchanting place to relax, forget your troubles, and indulge in gourmet fare.

Nona's was created in the fall of 1993 by restaurateur, Jonathan Enabnit, who designed a menu featuring meals that highlight fresh seafood, pasta creations topped with light, creamy sauces, savory risotto dishes, freshly made soups, and traditional sandwiches on homemade focaccia bread.

☐ *Carrot Soup à la Butterfield*

*This low calorie, low sodium soup is really quick and easy to pre-
pare. It's great as part of a multi-course dinner or as a light lunch entrée.
The soup's vivid orange color and sweet taste makes it a guest favorite at
Butterfield Bed & Breakfast's gourmet dinners. Even the housekeeper's
two-year-old loves eating his carrots this way.*

Makes 6 ample or 10 small servings.

2 teaspoons olive oil	1/2 teaspoon fresh grated
1 cup chopped onions	ginger
2 cups chopped leeks	Sour cream, whipped cream,
1 pound sweet carrots,	or nonfat yogurt for garnish
chopped medium	1 cup heavy cream, optional
9 cups chicken broth	

Heat olive oil in a large pot. Lightly sauté onions and leeks
until soft. Add carrots and chicken broth. Bring to a boil. Simmer
until carrots are softened, approximately 4 to 7 minutes. Allow to
cool slightly. Then, purée soup in batches in a blender. Return to
pot and simmer until hot.

When serving, top with a dollop of sour cream, whipped
cream, or nonfat yogurt, if desired. For a truly decadent (and higher
calorie) soup, stir in 1 cup of heavy cream.

⌂ Butterfield Bed and Breakfast
Julian, California

A stay in one of Butterfield Bed and Breakfast's four guest
rooms, each with a private bath and two with fireplaces, is guaranteed to be long remembered.

Owner and chef, Mary Trimmins, serves a lavish breakfast
in the garden gazebo during the warm summer months and in
the parlor when the chill makes its winter call. Dinner at the inn
begins with a garden soup, elegant salad, and chilled sorbet, followed by a tantalizingly tasty entrée.

Julian is a town for all seasons. Spring is filled with lilacs
and daffodils; summer offers warm days, apple blossoms; and
desert flowers, autumn is filled with red and gold fall leaves; and
winter is perfect for horse-drawn carriage rides and an occasional
dusting of snow.

⬚ *Homemade Carrot Soup*

Editor of Page One Cooks publications, Lynn Kerrigan, fortifies her family with delicious, home-cooked soups like this one. The bright color and sweet taste appeals even to those who shun vegetables.

Page One Cooks publishes culinary-related material including The Culinary Sleuth *newsletter;* 1001 Free Recipes; Smorgasbord of Cook's Newsletters, Magazines, and Journals; *and other cooking publications.*

Makes 6 servings.

1 onion
5 to 6 carrots
3 tablespoons butter
4 to 5 medium potatoes
2 to 3 cups water

2 cans beef or chicken stock (or
   3 bouillon cubes)
Salt & sugar (optional)
Chervil sprigs for garnish

Mince onion. Clean carrots and cut into fairly large cubes. Place onion and carrots in soup kettle with butter and cook, without browning, on very low heat for 1/2 hour. Peel and cube potatoes and add with 2 cups of water to soup. Bring to a boil and simmer for 1/2 hour.

If using canned stock, strain mixture and return to kettle, then stir in canned stock. (If using bouillon cubes, do not strain soup, simply add bouillon cubes to soup.) Gently boil for 5 or 6 minutes. Season to taste with salt and sugar. Garnish with sprigs of chervil.

☐ *Cream of Cauliflower Soup*

Linda Arnold, Grandview Lodge innkeeper, is a graduate home economist, chef, and cookbook author. She prepares first-rate meals that include locally grown fruits, vegetables, and herbs. All of the inn's breads, muffins, and biscuits are home baked and served with homemade jams, jellies, and relishes. Of course, she also makes soup from scratch. This soup is an all-time favorite served to guests of the lodge.

Makes about 12 cups.

3 tablespoons butter or oil
1 clove garlic
1 medium onion, coarsely chopped
3 ribs celery, coarsely chopped
1 carrot, coarsely chopped
1 head cauliflower, broken into large sections
2 tablespoons parsley
1/4 cup flour

8 cups chicken broth
Herbs for bouquet garni: 1 teaspoon peppercorns, 1 teaspoon dried tarragon, & 1 bay leaf
Salt to taste
1 cup evaporated milk or half-and-half
Freshly chopped tarragon (optional)

In a large soup pot, heat butter or oil. Add garlic, onion, celery, carrot, cauliflower, and parsley. Cook, covered, over medium heat for about 5 minutes, stirring occasionally. Stir in flour, coating vegetables. Add chicken broth. Bring to a boil. Put herbs for bouquet garni in a tea ball or tie in cheese cloth. Add to soup. Reduce heat, cover, and cook until vegetables are tender, about 15 minutes.

Remove vegetables from broth and purée in a blender or food processor. Return purée to soup pot. Heat and salt to taste. Stir in milk or half-and-half just before serving. Garnish each cup with freshly chopped tarragon, if desired.

Cauliflower Soups

⬜ *Coconut Cream of Celery Soup*

Meals at the Kilauea Lodge are served near the International Fire-place of Friendship, constructed in 1938 with stones from 32 countries around the world.

Serves 8 to 10 people.

10 cups chicken broth
3 pounds celery stalks, cubed
2 pounds russet potatoes,
   peeled & cubed
17 fluid ounces milk
1/2 cup heavy cream

1/2 cup coconut syrup
1-1/2 teaspoons celery salt
1 teaspoon white pepper
8 ounces unsalted butter, cut
   into 1/2-inch cubes
Parsley, finely chopped

Place broth in a 4-quart pot and bring to a boil. Purée celery and potato in a food processor until very fine. Add purée into boiling broth and beat with a whip for 2 minutes. Stir milk, cream, and coconut syrup into soup. Bring to a fast boil, then reduce heat to low and let simmer. Stir in celery salt and white pepper. Cover pot and let simmer for 40 minutes, stirring frequently.

Remove pot from stove. With a 2-ounce ladle, force liquid through a fine sift into a 4-quart bowl. Discard heavy purée in sift. Add butter to the soup bowl. Whip until butter is dissolved. Sprinkle a little parsley on each serving.

♻ Kilauea Lodge
Volcano Village, Hawaii

Innkeepers Lorna and Albert Jeyte lovingly tend their lodge on the Big Island of Hawaii. Each morning a full breakfast is served. Chef Albert learned to cook in France and offers a menu that reflects his European background and utilizes locally-grown fresh produce. Dinner specials include duck l'orange, lamb provencale, German sausage, and venison.

Kilauea Lodge guest rooms boast private baths, hot towel warmers, colorful comforters, and tropical flowers. The newest building on the property, Hale o Aloha, is equipped with central heating, a spacious common room, fireplace, and library.

☐ *Vermont Cheddar Cheese Soup*

Rabbit Hill Inn's Chef Russell Stannard sometimes varies this soup by adding ham, sun-dried tomatoes, grilled chicken, or croutons at presentation time.

Yields 12 servings.

6 tablespoons unsalted butter	4 cups chicken stock
1 cup diced onion	2 cups heavy cream
1/2 cup diced celery	1-1/2 pounds grated Vermont
1/2 cup diced carrot	Cheddar cheese
2 teaspoons minced garlic	1 teaspoon Worcestershire
8 tablespoons flour	sauce
1 teaspoon dry mustard	Salt & pepper to taste

Heat butter in a soup pot. Add diced onion, celery, carrot, and garlic. Sauté for 7 to 10 minutes. Sprinkle flour and mustard on top, reduce heat, and stir constantly for 10 minutes. Add chicken stock, 1 cup at a time, whisking to incorporate each time. Add heavy cream, bring to a boil, and simmer for 45 minutes.

Strain soup into another pot. Add cheese and Worcestershire sauce. Whisk to incorporate and melt. You may need to return this mixture to heat to help melt the cheese. If so, use a very low flame or a double boiler so soup doesn't burn. Season to taste with salt and pepper.

Cheese Soups

⬜ *Corn Chowder*

The Grandview Lodge dining room is innkeeper Linda Arnold's domain. This chowder recipe is one of her favorites. Author, Don Vandeventer, writes in his book, North Carolina Getaways: A Guide to Bed & Breakfasts & Inns, *"Her meals are truly fit for a king or queen."*

Makes about 12 cups.

3 tablespoons butter or oil
1 medium onion, coarsely
   chopped
2 ribs celery, coarsely chopped
2 carrots, coarsely chopped
2 cloves garlic
1 green pepper, divided
8 cups chicken broth
1 teaspoon dried thyme leaves

1 bay leaf
1 large potato, peeled &
   coarsely chopped
2 cups fresh or frozen corn,
   divided
Salt to taste
1-1/2 cups evaporated milk or
   half-and-half

In a large soup pot, heat butter or oil. Add onion, celery, carrots, garlic, and half of the green pepper. Cook, covered, over medium heat for about 5 minutes, stirring occasionally. Add chicken broth, herbs, potato, and 1 cup of the corn.

Cook over medium heat 10 to 15 minutes until vegetables are tender. Remove vegetables from broth and purée in a blender or food processor. Chop remaining half of the green pepper fine. Add to soup with remaining 1 cup of the corn and the purée. Cook for an additional 5 to 10 minutes. Taste and add salt if necessary. Stir in milk or half-and-half.

♧ Grandview Lodge
Waynesville, North Carolina

Grandview Lodge was built as a large farmhouse in the 1890s. In the 1940s, it was remodeled and made into an inn. Surrounded by apple orchards, grape arbors, and rhubarb patches, the lodge sits on 2-1/2 acres in the Great Smoky Mountains. For over 50 years, the lodge has been offering pleasant hospitality and exemplary home-cooked meals.

According to innkeepers, Stanley and Linda Arnold, "The lodge gives off a home-away-from-home feeling.....it's an ideal setting for a honeymoon, anniversary, reunion, or weekend getaway."

☐ *Grilled Sweet Corn Chowder with Herbed Pancake*

Monique Barbeau, executive chef of Fullers at the Sheraton Seattle Hotel & Towers, has won more cooking awards than you can shake a whisk at. A star-quality chef, she has been featured in many culinary publications and television programs, including In Julia's Kitchen with Master Chefs. Barbeau's soup recipe, like her, is filled with personality.

Serves 8 to 10.

8 ears fresh corn, peeled & husked
1/4 pound bacon, diced
1 onion, diced
1 carrot, diced
2 stalks celery, diced
2 potatoes, peeled & diced
1/2 teaspoon chipotle pepper, finely chopped

2 ounces white wine
4 cups chicken stock
6 ounces heavy cream, warmed
Salt & pepper to taste
Herbed Pancake (recipe follows)
Chopped chives & diced red pepper for garnish

Remove corn from 4 ears. Rub other 4 ears of corn with oil and grill until browned. Remove kernels from cob and keep separate, reserving 3 tablespoons for Herbed Pancakes.

In a saucepan, sauté bacon until lightly browned. Add diced vegetables and sauté until soft. Add chipotle pepper and wine and cook to reduce liquid by 2/3. Add chicken stock, potatoes, and corn. Simmer for 20 minutes or until potatoes are done. Purée half of the soup in a blender and return to pot. Add cream to soup and season with salt and pepper.

To serve, ladle into hot bowls, place 4 pieces of pancake into the middle of soup, and garnish with chives and red pepper.

Herbed Pancake

1 egg
3 ounces milk
3 ounces flour
1/4 teaspoon baking powder
1/2 ounce melted butter
1 teaspoon chopped chives

1/2 teaspoon chopped thyme
1/4 teaspoon chipotle pepper, chopped fine
3 tablespoons reserved grilled corn
2 ounces olive oil

Mix egg, milk, flour, baking powder, and butter together. Add herbs, pepper, and corn to batter. Let rest for 30 minutes. In a sauté pan, heat oil over medium heat. Place 1 tablespoon of batter in pan and cook for about 1 minute on each side. Remove from pan and cut into quarters.

Corn Soups

▯ Roasted Eggplant and Pepper Soup

Sous Chef Stephen Leonard's original soup recipe is among the best soup du jour creations on the menu of the Brassiere Bellevue, located in the Sutton Place Hotel.

Serves 4 to 6.

1 eggplant	**2 tablespoons Grainy Pomeray**
1 red pepper	**mustard**
1 yellow pepper	**1 teaspoon red curry paste**
1 green pepper	**1 tablespoon tomato paste**
1 onion, chopped	**1 teaspoon turmeric**
1 carrot, chopped	**Salt & pepper to taste**
3 cloves garlic, minced	**3 plum tomatoes, peeled &**
1/4 cup white wine	**diced**
4 cups chicken stock	**Chopped parsley for garnish**

Cut eggplant in half and roast until golden and soft. Cool, scoop meat out of skin, and set aside. Save 1/4 of the skin for garnish. Roast the 3 peppers until skin is evenly black. Place in a bowl and cover with plastic wrap to cool. When cool, peel skin, while saving juice from peppers. Dice fine and set aside.

In a large saucepan, sauté onions, carrots, and garlic until onion is translucent. Add white wine and reduce by half. Add chicken stock and reserved eggplant. Bring to a simmer. When carrots are cooked, stir in mustard, curry paste, and tomato paste. When blended, purée mixture and pass through a fine sieve.

Return to a simmer. Add turmeric and salt and pepper to taste. Mix in reserved peppers and diced tomato. Julienne the reserved eggplant skin and fry in oil to crisp. Drain and salt. To serve, ladle 6 ounces of soup into a bowl and garnish with fried eggplant at center. Sprinkle with chopped parsley.

ඌ The Sutton Place Hotel
Chicago, Illinois

Found in the heart of Chicago's posh Gold Coast neighborhood, The Sutton Place Hotel's location offers guests easy access to Chicago's major attractions, business district, and miles of Lake Michigan beachfront. The hotel's Brasserie Bellevue is a casual, friendly American eatery and seasonal, outdoor cafe. The restaurant, rated one of Chicago's best-kept secrets, serves innovative, "architecturally daring" cuisine, such as a tall teepee of chilled asparagus served atop tender vegetables.

⊓ Roasted Eggplant and Tomato Soup

Creative island cuisine is dominant at The Orchid at Mauna Lani. The club-like Grill Restaurant and Lounge features traditional grilled favorites with a light Northern Mediterranean flair and Hawaiian flavoring. The Cafe serves Pacific Island fare, local food favorites, and fitness cuisine in a relaxed, tropical setting. The Ocean Bar and Grill's beachside ambience provides excellent sunset cocktails, as well as salads, pizza, pasta, and a delightful children's menu.

Makes a huge pot.

8 pounds round eggplant	2 tablespoons rosemary,
8 pounds tomatoes	chopped
2 pounds whole garlic	3 quarts (12 cups) cream
Olive oil	Salt, pepper, & cayenne
3 pounds onions, julienne	pepper to taste
3 gallons chicken stock	Tomato concasse for garnish

Split eggplants, tomatoes, and garlic in half. Rub with olive oil and set cut side down on a baking sheet. Roast in a 350-degree oven until soft and golden brown. Take skin off and set aside.

Sweat onions in olive oil, then add eggplant, tomatoes, and garlic pulp. Sweat for 10 minutes. Stir in chicken stock. Simmer for 20 minutes. Mix in rosemary. Purée. Add cream to the desired consistency. Season to taste with salt, pepper, and cayenne. Garnish with tomato concasse.

☐ Roasted Eggplant with Wild Rice Soup

Thanks to Chef Tom Tassone, the food served on board the Queen Mary *is even better today than on the ship's 1936 maiden voyage. This soup recipe is one that satisfies the ship's current visitors.*

Makes 6 to 8 servings.

2 large eggplants	2 ounces tomato paste
Butter	4 cups chicken stock
1 teaspoon chopped onion	Roux to thicken as needed
1/4 teaspoon chopped shallot	1 cup cooked wild rice
1/4 teaspoon chopped garlic	Salt & pepper to taste
1 tablespoon chopped basil	

Peel eggplant and cut into small pieces. Roast with butter until soft and brown. In a large pot, briefly sauté eggplant with onion, shallot, garlic, and basil for 2 to 5 minutes. Add tomato paste and stir for 1 minute. Pour in chicken stock and bring to a boil. Then, lower heat and simmer for 45 minutes.

Add roux as needed to thicken. Simmer for 15 minutes more. Cool slightly and purée in a food processor or blender. Return to cooking pot and stir in cooked wild rice. Season to taste with salt and pepper.

ᖰ Queen Mary
Long Beach, California

The majestic *Queen Mary's* maiden voyage from Southampton, England to New York City occurred in 1936. The ship has performed many duties over her long history including transporting troops during World War 11 and taking countless transatlantic ocean voyages. Today, the *Queen Mary* sits along the shoreline in Long Beach. It's interior rivals other hotel and restaurant settings with its art deco elegance, period-style furnishings, and richly-appointed salons.

On-board restaurants include the Promenade Cafe, perfect for casual meals, The Chelsea, offering seafood specialities, and the elegant Sir Winston's serving award-winning California and Continental cuisine.

☐ *Roasted Garlic Soup*

The Rendezvous Inn & Restaurant proprietor and chef, Kim Badenhop, says it might be more proper to call this "sautéed" garlic soup because the garlic is "roasted" on top of the stove.

Makes 8 cups.

1 pound peeled garlic	1/2 teaspoon nutmeg
9-1/2 tablespoons butter	2-1/4 cups milk
1 teaspoon sugar	2-1/4 cups chicken stock,
2 teaspoons salt	unsalted
1/2 teaspoon ground white	2 cups cream
pepper	5 tablespoons flour
1 -1/4 cups white wine	Croutons for garnish
1 bay leaf	Chopped parsley for garnish

Coarsely chop garlic in a food processor. Melt 5-1/2 ounces of the butter in a heavy bottomed pan. Sauté garlic over low to medium heat until it just begins to brown. Add sugar, salt, and white pepper. Continue cooking until garlic is light brown. (Do not overcook garlic or it will lose its natural sweetness.) Add wine, bay leaf, and nutmeg. Bring to a boil and cook until wine is reduced by 2/3. Pour in milk, chicken stock, and cream. Return to a boil, then simmer for 15 to 20 minutes until garlic is tender.

Meanwhile, in a separate pan which is large enough to hold 4 cups of liquid, whisk flour and the remaining 4 tablespoons of butter together over medium heat. Cook, whisking continuously, until the mixture begins to take on some color. While whisking vigorously, begin to ladle soup into the flour mixture. Continue whisking and adding soup until half the soup has been added to the flour mixture. Then whisk flour mixture into soup. Bring to a simmer. Serve with a garnish of croutons and chopped parsley.

౿ The Rendezvous Inn & Restaurant
Fort Bragg, California

Hosts, Janice and Kim Badenhop, offer guests spacious, comfortable rooms in their historic, European-style country inn. The restaurant offers diners opportunity to indulge in a leisurely meal in an elegant setting.

Chef Kim's culinary background includes training in New York and France. Seasonal foods play an important part in Chef Kim's cuisine. The Rendezvous restaurants's menu changes monthly to reflect his passion for using fresh ingredients.

Garlic Soups

☐ *Gilroy Garlic Soup*

No one knows garlic better than garlic grower Don Christopher, owner of Christopher Ranch. One of the nation's largest fresh garlic growers, the business has been family owned and operated since 1956. Located in Gilroy, California, dubbed the Garlic Capitol of the World, the ranch now harvests 50 million tons of garlic a year.

The folks at Christopher Ranch are experts on cooking almost anything with garlic. Here's one of their soup recipes that's both simple and delicious.

Makes 8 servings.

1 large sweet onion, chopped
1 leek, white part only, washed
   well & chopped
3 tablespoons olive oil
8 cups chicken stock
2 large potatoes, peeled &
   chopped

15 cloves Christopher Ranch
   Whole Peeled Garlic
1 cup half-and-half
Salt & pepper to taste
1/2 cup chives, chopped

In a large pot, sauté onion and leek in olive oil until soft. Add chicken stock and bring to a boil. Add potatoes and garlic. Simmer for 1 hour.

Purée with half-and-half in a blender until smooth. Season to taste with salt and pepper. Garnish with chopped chives.

☐ *Roasted Garlic Potato Soup*

Kevin Koss is the chef at the newly-remodeled Jumpin' Jacks -- Cafe on the Water, located in the Sports Core, a spa and fitness club, in Kohler, Wisconsin. The restaurant's culinary philosophy is to create "interesting food for interesting people." Here's one of his speciality soups.

Makes about 32 cups.

1 tablespoon olive oil
1-1/2 cups diced white onions
3/4 cup diced celery
1/4 cup minced shallots
1/4 cup brown sugar
2 teaspoons dried thyme
10 large red potatoes, diced
1/3 cup flour

1 gallon vegetable stock
1 gallon skim milk
1 cup Roasted Garlic Purée
  (recipe follows)
1 whole bay leaf
Salt & black pepper to taste
Tabasco sauce (optional)

In a heavy-bottom stockpot, add olive oil, onions, celery, shallots, and brown sugar. Sauté until onions and sugar begin to caramelize. Add dried thyme and potatoes and continue to sauté. Dust with flour. Pour in vegetable stock and skim milk. Add Roasted Garlic Purée and bay leaf. Bring soup to a light simmer for at least 1 hour.

Remove bay leaf. Season to taste with salt and black pepper. For an extra kick, add a couple of shots of Tabasco sauce.

Roasted Garlic Purée

Peel fresh garlic cloves, coat with a small amount of olive oil, and wrap in tin foil. Bake at 350 degrees for 45 minutes to 1 hour, or until soft, sweet, and golden brown. Purée in a blender with some vegetable stock. Add to soup as directed.

☐ *Cream of Mushroom Soup*

The Orchid's traditional Cream of Mushroom Soup is updated with the inclusion of shiitake mushrooms

Makes 1 gallon.

3 pounds button mushrooms, minced
1-1/2 pounds shiitake mush- rooms, minced
2 ounces garlic, minced
1-1/2 pounds white or yellow onions, minced
4 ounces butter

2 cups white wine
1 cup sherry
3/4 gallon (12 cups) chicken stock
2 cups heavy cream
Roux or cornstarch
Salt & pepper to taste

Sauté mushrooms, garlic, and onions in butter until tender. Stir in white wine and sherry and cook over high heat to burn off alcohol. Add chicken stock and simmer for 20 minutes.

Finish soup with cream. Use a roux or cornstarch to thicken to desired consistency. Season to taste with salt and pepper.

⌂ The Orchid at Mauna Lani
Kohala Coast, Hawaii

The Orchid at Mauna Lani, on the Big Island of Hawaii, is a tropical resort nestled on 32 beachfront acres of the sunny Kohala Coast. The resort's ambience is relaxed while the level of service is what is expected at a world-class vacation destination. Guests enjoy swimming in a 10,000 square foot pool, a tennis match, playing golf on a 36-hole championship course, snorkeling, and many other island adventures.

Hawaii, the largest of the Hawaiian Island's, is an incredible oasis of discovery. Visitors delight in towering waterfalls, hikes through tropical rain forests, stargazing atop Mauna Kea, and viewing eruptions of the state's only active volcano by helicopter.

Cream of Mushroom Soup with Bleu Cheese

The L'Auberge dining room offers a casual bistro-style atmosphere and features the California cuisine of Chef Jamie West. The "bleu" cheese used in this soup recipe refers to one of the French "blue" cheeses such as Bleu d'Auvergne, Bleu de Salers, and Bleu de Bresse.

Makes 1 gallon.

1 cup butter
1 onion, 1/4-inch dice
2 stalks celery, 1/4-inch dice
1-1/2 pounds mushrooms, sliced
1 tablespoon garlic
1 cup flour
1 tablespoon dry mustard

1 tablespoon thyme, chopped
4 ounces white wine
3 quarts (12 cups) chicken stock
1 quart (4 cups) milk
4 ounces bleu cheese
Salt & white pepper to taste
Tabasco sauce to taste

Melt butter in pot. Add onions and celery and simmer on low heat for 10 minutes. Add mushrooms and garlic. Cook for 8 minutes until tender. Stir in flour, mustard, and thyme, and mix well. Pour in white wine and mix well. Add chicken stock, bring to a boil and simmer for 15 to 25 minutes until thick.

Stir in milk and cheese. Mix well. Season to taste with salt, white pepper, and Tabasco sauce.

L'Auberge Del Mar Resort & Spa
Del Mar, California

Overlooking the Pacific Ocean, the L'Auberge is positioned in the heart of Southern California's picturesque coastal village of Del Mar. The rare natural beauty of Del Mar is captivating. Long stretches of white sandy beach, marvelous year-round weather, and the relaxed pace of this seaside community proves a welcome retreat from big city life.

L'Auberge Del Mar Resort and Spa is the perfect place for one to retreat, refresh, and restore mind, body, and spirit with a wide variety of activities. Guests can make use of the Sports Pavilion equipment, attend exercise sessions in aerobics and yoga, workout with a personal trainer, take golf and tennis lessons, swim, engage in a vigorous scenic hike, and enjoy a sunrise walk along the beach. Exquisite skin and body treatments are also available at the state-of-the-art spa.

☐ Deer Valley's Mushroom & Wild Rice Soup

Deer Valley Resort's mid-mountain lodge, Silver Lake, houses three restaurants. The lodge's Executive Chef Clark Norris begins with savory classic dishes and adds contemporary foods to create wonderful updated meals. Old-fashioned mushroom soup has never been better than this upscale version with flavorful gourmet mushrooms.

Yields 1-1/2 gallons.

3 ounces butter
2 tablespoons garlic
2 onions, chopped
6 ounces chanterelle mushrooms
10 ounces shiitake mushrooms
3 ounces flour
6 quarts rich chicken stock
1 cup white wine
4 ounces dried porcini mushrooms, soaked in just
   enough water to cover

Juice of 2 lemons
1/4 cup sherry
3 tablespoons fresh thyme
Salt & freshly ground black
   pepper to taste
For garnish: 16 sliced shiitake
   mushroom caps, 20 halved
   chanterelle mushrooms, &
   1 teaspoon butter
1-1/2 cups wild rice, cooked

In an 8-quart soup pot, heat the butter and sauté garlic briefly. Add onions and cook until transparent. Add the chanterelle and shiitake mushrooms and cook over low heat until soft. Sprinkle in flour and cook this roux for about 10 minutes.

Meanwhile, heat the stock. When the roux is cooked, add stock to the mushroom mixture and whisk in well. Stir in wine. Chop the soaking porcini mushrooms. Rinse very well to remove all grit. Strain the soaking liquid through a double layer of cheesecloth. Add mushrooms and liquid to soup. Simmer for 1 hour.

Strain the soup into a serving vessel. Liquefy the remaining solids in a food processor and add them back to the soup. Season with lemon juice, sherry, thyme, salt, and pepper. Keep warm.

Prepare the garnish. Sauté sliced shiitake and chanterelle mushrooms in 1 teaspoon butter until tender. Add to soup with the wild rice.

⊂⊃ Deer Valley Resort
Park City, Utah

Deer Valley Resort, situated in the Rocky Mountains, receives an average of 300 inches of "The Greatest Snow on Earth" each year, offering some of the best skiing in the West. Whether you're a beginner or a seasoned expert, the three mountains of Deer Valley provide over 1,100 acres of skiing pleasure.

Deer Valley has something for everyone. The rustic elegance of the resort's two day-use lodges are a welcome rest area for skiers. Overnight vacationers can chose from an enticing array of luxurious accommodations from deluxe hotel rooms to three or four bedroom condominiums with private hot tubs.

Some say that the food alone makes the trip to Deer Valley worthwhile. Try catering to a party of 5,000 people, in all forms of ski attire, when your restaurants are almost two miles above sea level, in six different locations. That is, in a nutshell, the job of Deer Valley's food and beverage department, expertly guided by its director, Julie Wilson. Her goal is to offer guests the best culinary experience at *any* altitude. What you'll find in any one of the resort's restaurants is sumptuous buffets and innovative meals prepared exclusively from fresh ingredients by skilled chefs. The selection and quality of food is unprecedented at a ski resort.

Mushroom Soups

🗍 Wild Mushroom Cappuccino

Under the expert guidance of Chef de Cuisine Christophe Barbier, Mark's Restaurant, located in The Mark hotel in New York City, is a dining spot with several culinary personalities.

Breakfast offers a generous selection of traditional popular dishes joined by one or two signature items. The lunch menu consists of grilled meats, sandwiches, salads, and a three-course prix fixe menu. The evening meal features dishes that showcase the culinary staff's inventiveness, technique, and sophistication. This soup, created by Chef Barbier, is one of the signature dishes.

Makes 8 servings.

1 cup peeled shallots, finely
   sliced
3 cloves garlic, chopped
2 tablespoons butter
2 pounds wild mushrooms
   (such as shiitakes, oysters,
   morels, portabellos)
1 bunch sage, tied in a bouquet

2 Idaho potatoes, peeled &
   cut up
4 cups chicken stock
1 cup heavy cream
Salt & pepper to taste
1 cup steamed milk
1 pinch cinnamon

In a soup pot, sweat shallots and garlic in butter. Roughly chop mushrooms and add to pot. Cook for 2 minutes. Add sage bouquet, potatoes, chicken stock, and heavy cream. Cook for 20 minutes.

Blend soup. Strain through a fine sifter. Adjust seasoning with salt and pepper. Serve hot soup in coffee cups covered with seamed milk and sprinkled with cinnamon.

☐ *Woodland Mushroom Broth*

Chef John Petzold was born in the rugged terrain of Alaska and raised in the heart of the gentle farmlands of the Midwest. It was there he began hiking at an early age and reveled in the bounty of the land. At almost the same time, he developed an interest in cooking and treating food preparation with an innate respect for the ingredients and their mouth-watering flavors. The chef favors natural American cuisine. His goal is to wed the finest standards of food preparation and add to them "the subtle enhancement of foods with flavors drawn from the ethnic groups who settled the country."

Makes 12 servings.

1 large strip kombu (seaweed)
3 quarts cold water
4 to 5 cups kadzuo (dried bonita fish flakes)
Tofu
Oil
12 whole spring onions
1 pound shiitake mushrooms (whole caps)
1 pound mitake mushrooms (leave in bunches)
1 pound honshimiji mushrooms
1 pound oyster mushrooms (stems removed)
4 tablespoons sake (Japanese rice wine)
4 tablespoons mirin (slightly syrupy rice wine)
2 tablespoons soy sauce
1 cup white miso (mild white fermented soy bean paste)

Place kombu in water and bring to a simmer. Remove kombu when tender. Add kadzuo and steep for 30 seconds. Strain, cool, and reserve stock. Cut tofu into large 1-inch slices and sauté in a little oil until golden brown. Remove and set aside. Sauté onions and the four types of mushrooms over high heat for 1 minute. Add sake, mirin, and soy sauce. Cook to reduce liquid.

Add reserved stock. Bring to a boil, then remove from heat. Strain miso into soup and whisk. Add tofu. Do not boil kombu, kadzuo, or miso as a bitter flavor will result.

↻ The Jefferson
Washington, D.C.

The Jefferson hotel belongs to The Lancaster Group, which is comprised of unique luxury properties with great character and personal service. The Jefferson caters to the business traveler by providing each guest room an arsenal of services including a private line dedicated fax machine, multiple two-line speaker phones, VCRs, stereo CD players, and fully stocked bars. Each of the properties feature as their trademark an all concierge staffed front desk.

Mushroom Soups

🍞 *Creamy Five Onion Soup*

Few restaurants have received the international recognition that has become a tradition for the Steak House at Harrah's Casino. The unique presentation of this classic soup makes it a favorite.

Makes 4 servings.

4 large Spanish onions (5-inch
  in diameter)
1 red onion
2 leeks
1 bunch green onions
2 ounces shallots
3 ounces butter
1 teaspoon sweet basil
3 ounces flour

2 cups beef stock or bouillon
2 ounces Burgundy wine
2 ounces Chablis wine
2 teaspoons black pepper
1 cup heavy whipping cream
4 French bread croutons
4 ounces Swiss cheese
4 ounces Gruyère cheese

Cut off the tops of 4 Spanish onions about 1/2-inch down. Hollow out the center without breaking through the sides or bottom (leave about 3 layers of onion on the sides and bottom). Set aside. Dice removed onion pieces along with the other onions.

Melt butter in a soup pot over medium heat. Add all chopped onions and sweet basil. Sauté until tender. Do not brown onions. Add flour to make a roux. Cook for 5 minutes, stirring constantly. Pour in beef stock and continue stirring until smooth. Add wines and black pepper and cook for an additional 20 minutes. Stir in heavy cream and cook for 15 minutes.

Place hollow "onion bowls" in a 400-degree oven for 10 minutes. Remove and fill with hot soup. Top with crouton and cheeses. Return to oven or broiler until cheese melts to a golden brown.

🍳 Harrah's Casino
Reno, Nevada

The staff at Harrah's Steak House is renowned for superb and friendly service, and the restaurant's captains and servers excel in table-side cooking. Savory specialities include rack of lamb with a herb crust topped with a pine nut-pinot noir sauce, and steak Diane. From the broiler, there's filet mignon, swordfish, and double-cut lamb chops, all cooked to order. To enrich the taste buds, an extensive selection of fine wines and delectable desserts are available to top off any meal.

☐ *Tuscan Three Onion Soup with Grilled Bread & Shaved Parmesan*

Joanne Weir, a well-seasoned chef, emphasizes foods of the Mediterranean in her book, From Tapas to Meze *(Crown Publishers, 1994). Like this soup, many of the cookbook's dishes, begin with simple ingredients of humble origins that satisfy the soul as well as the body. The third onion in this recipe is garlic, a member of the onion family.*

Makes 6 servings.

4 tablespoons extra-virgin olive oil	2 cloves garlic, peeled
4 large yellow onions, thinly sliced	4 tablespoons Balsamic vinegar
4 medium-size leeks, 1/4-inch dice	1 cup Chianti or Zinfandel red wine
4 ounces pancetta (Italian bacon), 1/4-inch dice	Salt and freshly ground black pepper to taste
6 cups chicken stock	4-ounce chunk Parmesan cheese
6 slices rustic, country-style bread, 3/4-inch thick, toasted	2 tablespoons freshly chopped Italian parsley

Heat olive oil in a large soup pot over medium heat. Add the onions, leeks, and pancetta. Cook until the onions are soft and pancetta is a light golden color, about 15 minutes. Add chicken stock and simmer for 30 minutes. Meanwhile, rub toasted bread with a clove of garlic. Place one piece of bread in the bottom of each serving bowl.

To serve, add vinegar, wine, salt, and pepper to soup pot. Ladle soup onto the toasted bread in serving bowls. Shave 4 or 5 thinly sliced pieces of Parmesan cheese on top of each. Garnish with chopped parsley and serve immediately.

ꙮ Joanne Weir
San Francisco

Joanne Weir is a fourth generation professional cook whose passion is teaching. A San Francisco-based chef, author, and cooking instructor, she has taught across the United States, Canada, Australia, and New Zealand. Ms. Weir has written cookbooks for the Williams-Sonoma/Time Life series and articles for many noted culinary magazines such as *Bon Appétit, Food and Wine,* and *Fine Cooking.* She has been honored with the Cooking Teacher Award of Excellence during the 1996 International Association Cooking Professional Awards.

Onion Soups

☐ *Parsnip Vichyssoise*

The Governor's Inn proprietors, Charlie and Deedy Marble, make many of their guests favorite recipes available in two cookbooks: A Box of Culinary Secrets from the Inn's Kitchen *and* From the Inn's Kitchen. *Parsnips are a favorite root vegetable at the inn. Diners love the sweet, nutty flavor of this soup. Deedy Marble, makes another of her soups, Sweet Potato Vichyssoise by substituting eight peeled sweet potatoes for the parsnips.*

Makes approximately 8 to 10 servings.

2 large leeks, white part only,
   halved lengthwise & sliced
   crosswise 1/2-inch thick
3 pounds parsnips, peeled &
   cut into chunks
3 medium boiling potatoes,
   peeled & cut into chunks
1 large onion, halved & thinly
   sliced
3 large cloves garlic, crushed
2 tablespoons light brown
   sugar

1 teaspoon ground cardamon
3 cups chicken stock
3 cups white wine
1 stick sweet, unsalted butter,
   cut into small pieces
1/4 cup fresh lemon juice
2-1/2 cups half-and-half cream
2-1/2 cups heavy cream
Salt & freshly ground pepper
Whole chives for garnish

Preheat oven to 350 degrees. In a large roasting pan, combine leeks, parsnips, potatoes, onion, and garlic. Sprinkle with sugar and cardamon and stir to combine. Pour 2 cups of the chicken stock and 3 cups white wine over vegetables and dot with butter. Cover tightly with aluminum foil and braise for two hours until vegetables are very tender. Lift the foil and stir vegetables occasionally. Transfer vegetables and any liquid to a large saucepan. Add the remaining 1 cup of chicken broth and lemon juice and bring to a boil. Reduce heat and simmer, covered, for 20 minutes.

Working with small batches, blend soup in a food processor or blender. Cool, add creams, and reheat, stirring occasionally, until warmed through. Do not boil. Taste for seasoning. Serve garnished with snipped chives and chive blossoms.

Summer Sorrel and Sweet Pea Soup

The Lemaire restaurant is located in what used to be the original ladies' parlors of the 100-year-old Jefferson Hotel in Richmond, Virginia. Chef Mark Langenfeld leads a talented culinary team who specialize in updated Southern cooking and Thomas Jefferson's culinary passions.

Chef Langenfeld has thoroughly researched and become an expert on what he calls (Thomas) Jeffersonian cuisine. According to an article written by Langenfeld, in Culinary Trends, *Jefferson "profoundly influenced the culinary practices of Americans for years. In fact, he brought about changes that affect our eating habits today."*

Langenfeld explains that Jefferson believed in healthful quantities of vegetables and fruits; enjoyed spices, like cayenne, from the Caribbean; favored French wines over whiskey; was fascinated with French cuisine and cooking with wine; and brought a recipe from Paris called French custard, what we now know as ice cream. Jefferson promoted one of his favorite vegetables, the tomato, was once thought to be poisonous, and was responsible for introducing sesame seeds to the U.S.

A man ahead of his time, Thomas Jefferson encouraged healthy eating and responsible drinking. Today, many Lemaire menu selections are inspired by Jefferson's beliefs, including the following recipe.

Serves 8.

1 cup diced sweet white Vidalia onions
1 cup diced young spring onions
1 cup diced celery
1 cup diced domestic mushrooms
8 ounces butter
5 cups fresh (or frozen) sweet peas
1/2 cup flour
5 cups good fresh chicken stock
1 cup white wine
2 leaves sorrel chiffonade

Sauté onions, celery, and mushrooms in butter until soft. Add sweet peas and cook until al dente. Lightly dust with flour and slowly brown for 5 minutes. Whisk chicken stock and white wine into vegetables quickly and simmer for 20 minutes. Garnish with a sorrel leaf chiffonade.

☐ *Potage of Minted Snap Peas and Greens*

The New Blueberry Hill Cookbook *is filled with fabulous recipes from the creative cooks whose superb dishes have graced the inn's tables since 1971. Some are sinfully rich, some deliciously sophisticated, all are plain delicious. Fresh garden vegetables are used in this soup.*

Serves 6.

6 ounces fresh spinach, washed, stemmed & torn

6 ounces (1 small bunch) watercress, washed & stemmed

4 tablespoons sweet butter

2 large yellow onions, finely chopped

3-1/2 cups chicken stock

12 ounces sugar snap peas, strings removed, rinsed, & dried

1 small bunch fresh mint, washed, stemmed, & dried

1 cup light cream

Salt & freshly ground black pepper to taste

Mint leaves for garnish

Steam spinach and watercress until wilted. Drain well and squeeze out any excess liquid. Set aside. Melt butter in a large heavy saucepan over medium heat. Add chopped onion, cover and cook over low heat until lightly colored, about 20 minutes.

Pour chicken stock into the onions and stir in peas, spinach, and watercress. Bring to a boil. Reduce heat and simmer, partially covered, for about 15 minutes, or until peas are tender. Add mint to saucepan, cover, and simmer for another 5 minutes.

Strain soup, reserving liquid. Transfer solids to the bowl of a food processor fitted with a steel blade. Add 1 cup of cooking stock and process until smooth. Return the puréed soup to cooking pot. Add cream and about 1 additional cup of the reserved cooking liquid. Add more liquid if soup is too thick.

Season to taste with salt and pepper. Simmer gently until heated through. Serve immediately, garnished with mint leaves.

↻ Blueberry Hill
Goshen, Vermont

Blueberry Hill, a beautifully restored 1813 country inn surrounded by English-style gardens and a spring-fed pond, is nestled at the foot of Romance Mountain. The inn's setting offers seasonal cross-country skiing and 40 miles of trails for walking, hiking, and biking. Tony Clark, the inn's proprietor, welcomes guests to an unhurried four-course dinner of simple and elegant meals.

▯ *Virginia Peanut Soup*

Lemaire, The Jefferson's fine dining establishment, is named for Thomas Jefferson's White House maitre d'hotel who introduced the art of cooking with wine to America. Chef Mark Langenfeld's menu reflects Jefferson's keen interest in gourmet dining.

Serves 8.

3 stalks celery, diced	4 cups good chicken stock
2 carrots, diced	3/4 cup peanut butter
1 medium onion, diced	1 cup heavy cream
3/4 cup butter	1/2 cup Frangelico (a hazelnut-
2 cups peanuts	flavored cordial)
Flour to thicken soup	Salt & pepper to taste

Cook diced celery, carrots, and onion in a 2-quart stockpot over medium heat with butter and peanuts until vegetables are tender, about 10 to 12 minutes. Add flour and cook for 5 to 8 minutes until lightly browned, stirring often. Whisk in chicken stock. Then, reduce heat and cook until thickened, about 10 to 12 minutes, stirring often.

Mix in peanut butter and purée soup in a food processor or blender. Finish with cream and Frangelico. Season to taste with salt and pepper.

⌘ The Jefferson Hotel
Richmond, Virginia

The Jefferson Hotel has been at the hub of Richmond social life since its opening over a century ago. Through the years, the hotel, named for America's third president, has set the tone for impressive accommodations and five-diamond dining.

The rotunda is one of the most memorable lobbies in the country, boasting faux marble pillars supporting a 70-foot ceiling that's embellished with multi-color and gold-leaf designs. The highlight of the room is the double wide, sweeping marble staircase. Legend has it this staircase was the model for the famous one featured in *Gone with the Wind*.

The Palm Court is now the registration area and features the original bellman's desk, nine original stained-glass side-windows, and an impressive marble statue of Thomas Jefferson, which was created for the hotel in the late 1800s.

☐ *Roasted Sweet Pepper Bisque with Papaya Relish and Lemon Aïoli*

Chef Brent Wertz draws upon his well-rounded expertise in American cooking to tantalize the guests of the Mohonk Mountain House, a 275-room Victorian-era lodge. Wholesome foods prepared with fresh ingredients are the hallmark of dining at Mohonk. For those who prefer a menu of health-conscious meals, the retreat offers an alternative "Sound Choice" menu selection. Cookouts overlooking the lake are a sensational seasonal treat.

Yields 1/2 a gallon.

4 red peppers, roasted, peeled
& seeded
4 green peppers, roasted,
peeled & seeded
4 yellow peppers, roasted,
peeled & seeded
4 ounces onions, diced
2 ounces carrots, diced
2 ounces celery, diced
2 cloves garlic, diced

2 ounces safflower oil
2 ounces mixed chopped herbs
(oregano, chives, basil,
marjoram, etc.)
12 cups chicken stock
Lemon juice, malted vinegar,
salt, & pepper to taste
Papaya & Red Onion Relish
(recipe follows)
Lemon Aïoli (recipe follows)

Sauté peppers, onions, carrots, celery, and garlic in safflower oil. Add herbs and chicken stock and cook until liquid is reduced by 1/3. Purée soup. Finish with lemon juice, malted vinegar, salt, and pepper to taste. Top with a dollop of Papaya & Red Onion Relish and drizzle with Lemon Aïoli.

Papaya & Red Onion Relish

1 papaya, diced small
1/2 small red onion, diced
small
1 green onion, diced small

1/4 jicama, diced small
Juice of 1 lime
1/2 bunch cilantro, chopped
Salt & pepper to taste

Combine all ingredients and fold together.

Lemon Aïoli

1 egg yolk
1/2 teaspoon garlic
1 teaspoon Dijon mustard

4 ounces extra-virgin olive oil
1/2 lemon, juiced
Salt & pepper to taste

Place egg yolk, garlic, and mustard into blender. Add oil slowly with machine on low speed. Finish with lemon juice and salt and pepper to taste. Adjust consistency with hot water if too thick.

Mohonk Mountain House
New Paltz, New York

Imagine sleeping in a castle overlooking a crystal clear lake. Mohonk Mountain House offers thousands of acres of unspoiled scenery. Since 1869, Mohonk, a National Historic Landmark destination resort, has hosted guests in a turreted Victorian castle.

Tucked away at the top of the Shawangunk ridge is Lake Mohonk, a half-mile long, sixty-foot deep sky water lake. Innkeeper, Albert K. Smiley, great-grandnephew of Mohonk's founder, encourages guests to enjoy the many features of the landscaped grounds and the adjoining 6,300-acre Mohonk Preserve.

The resort offers planned theme programs throughout the year such as Jazz on the Mountain, Garden Dreams, Swing Dance Weekend, and a Film Weekend: Classic Cartoons and Animation. Whether interested in sports, recreational activities, history, nature, theme programs, or simply in need of a relaxing holiday, Mohonk caters to all desires.

☐ Roast Potato and Asparagus Bisque

The Four Season's cuisine highlights the abundance of local fresh fruits and vegetables, and freshly-caught fish and seafood. Specialities include a variety of West Indian fare, grilled fish and meat, lobster dishes, and homemade soups.

Makes 6 to 8 servings.

2 pounds baby red-skin
  potatoes
Salt, white pepper, & olive oil
  for seasoning
1 medium onion, diced
3 celery stalks, diced
3 garlic cloves
3 tablespoons olive oil

2 pounds fresh asparagus,
  chopped
2 cups white wine
1/4 cup vermouth
6 cups chicken broth
2 cups heavy cream
1/4 pound unsalted butter,
  softened

Season potatoes with salt, pepper, and olive oil. Roast in a 375-degree oven for 25 minutes. Meanwhile, sauté onions, celery, and garlic in olive oil over medium-high heat for 2 minutes. Add asparagus and sauté for 2 more minutes. Pour in white wine and cook until liquid is reduced by half. Add vermouth and reduce liquid by half again. Add roasted potatoes and chicken stock. Lower heat and simmer for 20 minutes. Add cream and return to a boil. Remove soup from heat and purée in a blender, taking care not to splash hot liquid out of blender. Pour soup back into pot and whisk in butter. Season to taste with salt and white pepper.

⟳ Four Seasons Resort
Nevis, West Indies

The restaurants and lounges at the Four Seasons Resort Nevis are designed to insure maximum exposure to the outdoors, while creating the ambiance of a West Indian plantation great house.

The Grill Room is an open-air restaurant overlooking the Caribbean Sea which boasts a magnificent sunset view. Located upstairs in the Great House, the restaurant is decorated with brightly colored Caribbean tiles and ceiling fans.

The second-floor Dining Room restaurant, with commanding ocean views, is accented with a wooden-plank plantation-style floor, a high open-rafter planked ceiling, and stone fireplace.

☐ *Potato-Ramp Soup*

So, you ask, what the heck is a ramp? According to The View from Cataloochee *newsletter, it's a wild onion, native to North Carolina's mountain's rich woods. Ramps look a lot like the more commonly-known scallion or green onion. The gathering season is short, from early April to early May. To prepare, they are first cleaned, then chopped into small pieces, and parboiled in lightly salted water with a teaspoon of vinegar (to kill the ramps' powerful smell) for about 5 minutes. Then, the traditional way to cook ramps is to fry them in bacon fat and gradually add enough eggs to make the dish green and yellow. They can be cooked and eaten with cornbread and fried potatoes or fish. You can also make a very tasty hot potato soup, like this one.*

Serves 10.

6 medium potatoes, diced
12 ramps, diced
3 stalks celery, diced
1 gallon water

1 tablespoon chicken base
2 cups half-and-half
Salt & pepper to taste

Combine all ingredients in a soup pot. Cook for 30 minutes on medium heat until soup thickens.

ᑐ Cataloochee Ranch
Maggie Valley, North Carolina

General Manager, Tim Rice, describes the Cataloochee Ranch philosophy this way: "Cataloochee Ranch has always catered to families, providing them a comfortable place to visit in a beautiful setting. They eat delicious food, ride, or hike where they like, or just sit and read."

The meals at the ranch center around southern Appalachian regional cuisine. To support this country fare the staff makes weekly shopping trips to local farmers' markets and nearby farms to taste, select, and purchase fresh mountain-grown products for use by the ranch chefs. A special emphasis is placed on serving fresh fruits and vegetables, homemade breads, desserts, jellies, preserves, and native mountain delicacies like ramps.

⬜ *Acorn Squash and Turnip Soup*

Dux, The Peabody Orlando's signature restaurant, is an exquisite room adorned with a series of paintings depicting the property's cherished mascots, North American mallard ducks. An elegant decor of muted gold and bronze tones, a selection of fine wines, and expertly-prepared global-American cuisine are the carefully chosen ingredients that make an evening at Dux one that's long remembered.

Makes 8 servings.

1-1/2 pounds acorn squash, halved & seeded
4-1/2 tablespoons unsalted butter
1 pound leeks, white part only, coarsely chopped
1 medium onion, coarsely chopped
2 small carrots, grated
1 clove garlic, chopped
1 teaspoon sugar
3/4 pound turnips, peeled & cut into eighths
6 cups chicken stock
1/2 teaspoon salt
1/4 teaspoon freshly ground white pepper
1/8 teaspoon ground coriander
Crème fraîche or sour cream for garnish

Preheat oven to 375 degrees. Place acorn squash in a foil-lined baking pan. Rub exposed areas with 1/2 tablespoon of the butter and bake until fork-tender, about 1 hour.

Meanwhile, in a large flameproof casserole, melt remaining 4 tablespoons of butter over moderate heat. Add leeks, onions, carrots, and garlic. Sprinkle sugar over all. Reduce heat to low, cover and cook until vegetables are soft, about 20 minutes.

Add turnips, 2-1/2 cups of the stock, salt, white pepper, and coriander. Simmer, uncovered, over moderate heat until turnips are tender, about 25 minutes.

When squash is cooked, scoop out flesh and add it to the casserole. Purée soup, in batches if necessary, in a blender or food processor. Return to pot and stir in remaining 3-1/2 cups stock. Heat through. Serve with a dollop of crème fraîche or sour cream.

▯ *Butternut and Acorn Squash Soup*

This wonderful festive soup is served in an acorn squash. Chef Jim Makinson suggests substituting water for the chicken stock if you want to make vegetarian soup.

Makes 6 servings.

1 butternut squash to yield
  about 1-1/2 pounds peeled
1 acorn squash, peeled
2 ounces onion
2 ounces leek
2 ounces whole butter
6 cups good chicken stock

Salt & pepper to taste
1 acorn squash for serving
  bowl
For garnish: 1 ounce julienne
  leeks, 1 ounce crème fraîche,
  & chopped chives

Cut butternut and acorn squash into rough dice. Cut onions and white of leeks into rough dice. Sauté onions and leeks in 1/4 ounce of the butter. Add squash and chicken stock. (Chicken base and water may be substituted for the chicken stock.) Cook soup for 20 minutes until squash is soft. Soup should be fairly thick before you purée. Place mixture in a blender to purée. Add rest of butter and season to taste.

To prepare serving bowl, cut top off and shave just enough off the bottom of the acorn squash so it will sit up without tipping over. Remove seeds and steam, covered, until soft. Place acorn squash in oven with a small amount of water on the tray and bake for 10 to 12 minutes. Cut leeks into a fine julienne (hairlike) and sauté. Mix crème fraîche with chives. Serve soup, family-style, in acorn squash. Top with leeks and crème fraîche.

⌓ Loews Ventana Canyon Resort
Tuscon, Arizona

Perched on a plateau high above the city, Loews Ventana Canyon Resort boasts a tantalizing array of culinary samplings and extraordinary views. The Ventana Room, featuring daily prix fixe selections and a seasonal menu, is perfectly positioned for views of the Tuscon skyline or the 80-foot canyon waterfall. The Canyon Café has a casual rustic ambiance offering mountain, pool, and waterfall views. Flying V Bar & Grill, a favorite golfer watering hole, offers a relaxed Southwestern lodge feeling and optional al fresco dining. Bill's Grill, an informal poolside eatery, is famous for its mesquite-grilled burgers, chicken, and sausage.

☐ Cream Ogwissimanabo Butternut with Cucumber and Honey

The Holiday Inn Toronto Airport hotel and restaurants feature dining facilities to suit all tastes. This soup is one of Executive Chef Max Benz's most popular. The rich creamy taste is from a white roux.

Makes approximately 30 portions.

5 pound butternut squash
2 medium onions, chopped
2 ounces butter
2 ounces garlic, chopped
2 gallons chicken stock

Salt & pepper to taste
1 medium cucumber
8 ounces roux (flour & butter
  mixture)
2 ounces honey

Peel squash and dice. In a large stockpot, sauté squash and onions together in butter until tender. Add garlic and chicken stock. Cook for 2 hours on medium heat.

Season to taste with salt and pepper. Peel cucumber, remove seeds and slice very fine. Thicken soup with roux. Add cucumber and honey and serve.

☐ Curried Butternut, Sweet Potato & Cheddar Soup

The Montpelier dinner menu, orchestrated by Chef Stuart Jones, changes daily. Diners have recently indulged in Avocado Fan with Melon Pearls, Lobster Ravioli with Dill Sauce, Mahi Mahi Fillet with Saffron and Chive Sauce, and Iced Pistachio Parfait in Tulip Basket.

Serves 12.

5 butternut squash
5 sweet potatoes
3 cloves garlic
1 onion
2 stalks celery
2 leeks
Oil for sautéing
2 tablespoons curry powder

Fresh coriander
1 gallon chicken stock
1/2 pound grated Cheddar
   cheese
For garnish: croutons, fresh
   coriander, & 1/2 cup heavy
   cream (optional)

Peel squash and sweet potatoes. Chop and set aside. Wash and chop remaining vegetables. Sauté vegetables in oil in a hot pan until tender. Add curry powder and coriander. Add squash and sweet potatoes. Sweat for 3 to 4 minutes. Pour in chicken stock and bring to a boil. Simmer until potatoes are cooked, about 45 minutes. Place in liquidizer and blend with cheese. Return to a clean pan. Serve garnished with croutons, fresh coriander, and a whirl of cream, if desired.

☙ Montpelier Plantation Inn
Nevis, West Indies

Vacationers seeking tropical hospitality and classical cuisine should check out the Montpelier Plantation Inn. The 17 rooms of the secluded inn are light and airy and recently refurbished in a fresh, clean tropical style. Visitors can spend part of the day at the inn's private beach, then pursue other activities including tennis, golf, freshwater swimming, windsurfing, snorkeling, scuba diving, deep sea fishing, and horseback riding.

Several Nevisian and European chefs create fabulous meals with fresh local produce and bounty from the sea including fresh lobster. The morning meal is served in the light and airy flower-filled Breakfast Room. The Lunch Terrace offers dining a la carte and the outside Dining Terrace gives views past floodlit palm trees to the distant lights of St. Kitts.

☐ *Christophene Soup*

Owner and chef of Rawlins, Claire Rawson, makes delightful, easy-to-prepare soups for her guests. Christophenes are a popular squash-like vegetable, pale green in color and pear shaped. They may be found in Latin-American markets under the name chayote. This delicate soup is suitable for serving before a hearty meal or as a middle course.

Serve 4 to 6.

2 tablespoons butter
1 large onion, peeled & chopped
1/2 leek, chopped
3 medium christophene, peeled & sliced (care must be taken when handling as there are sometimes tiny prickles on the skin)

1 tablespoon fresh thyme, chopped
1 tablespoon fresh parsley, chopped
Salt & white pepper to taste
4 cups chicken or vegetable stock
2 tablespoons fresh chives, chopped, for garnish

Heat butter in a saucepan over medium heat. Gently sauté onion and leek, being careful not to let them brown. Add christophene, herbs, seasoning, and stock. Bring to a boil and simmer for about 30 minutes or until christophene is tender. Purée christophene in a food processor with leeks and herbs, adding stock gradually. When ready to serve, reheat soup, ladle into bowls, and scatter freshly chopped chives over the top.

⌂ Rawlins Plantation Hotel & Restaurant
St. Kitts, West Indies

Rawlins Plantation was formerly one of 300 sugar estates that operated in St. Kitts. *New York Magazine* calls the plantation ".....one of the most appealing inns in the West Indies....." Perhaps it's the tranquility that makes it so special.....or the gentle breezes and swaying palms. These assets, combined with some superb dining, all contribute to such adulation.

Most of the ingredients used in the restaurant's kitchen are from the plantation's own gardens or from local farmers. Although choice cuts of meat are imported, the fish and seafood are caught and delivered fresh by local fisherman.

⬜ *Spicy Seasonal Squash Soup*

The Chaddsford Winery is a Great Tastes of Pennsylvania festival participant. Proprietors, Eric and Lee Miller, suggest serving Chaddsford Chardonnay with this soup, featured in a 1994 Bon Appétit dinner.

Serves 8.

2 (8-inch) butternut squash
2 tablespoons olive oil
8 cups good chicken stock,
  preferably unsalted

1 teaspoon salt
1 medium jalapeño pepper,
  finely diced
4 large pinches saffron

Peel squash and cut the neck ends into 1/2- to 3/4-inch slices. Brown these quickly in a large, heavy skillet in olive oil, just until they have a crispy brown skin. While they are cooking, cut the rest of the squash into wedges and place in a large saucepan with 4 cups of the chicken stock. Cook over medium heat. When the slices are crispy, dice and add to rest of the cooking squash. Add salt and 1/2 of the jalapeño pepper. Continue cooking for 15 to 20 minutes until squash is tender enough to be mashed easily. Remove squash from heat and mash with fork or potato masher until squash is a pulpy consistency with some small lumps.

About 5 minutes before serving, complete soup by adding 4 cups of hot chicken stock, 4 large pinches saffron, and rest of jalapeño pepper to the purée. Mix gently, heat until warm, and serve immediately. The red strands of saffron should be floating on top along with bits of green jalapeño pepper. The soup looks best if served in large, shallow, clear bowls.

⚘ Great Tastes of Pennsylvania Wine & Food Festival
Lake Harmony, Pennsylvania

Each year the Resort at Split Rock hosts the Great Tastes of Pennsylvania Wine & Food Festival. Set in the beautiful Pocono Mountains, the two-day outdoor celebration features the state's finest wineries offering tastes of their latest vintages and award-winning premium wines.

Musical entertainment ranges from country and blues to folk songs and reggae. Crafts and art work from dozens of artisans are exhibited, and food purveyors offer various delectable menus. Small fry delight in pony rides, face painting, and other special activities.

The Resort also hosts the annual Great Brews of America, a classic beer festival held in November.

☐ *Gingered Pumpkin Bisque*

Chef Joseph Nartowicz has developed a reputation as a chef with a natural touch. A longtime believer in healthful foods, he partners with several local farms to provide fresh produce daily. His commitment to natural, organic, whole foods took center stage when he developed a new menu for Cafe Rouge, Boston Park Plaza Hotel's main restaurant.

Yields 6 servings.

1/2 teaspoon chopped fresh ginger	4 cups heavy cream
1-1/2 ounces white wine	3 ounces wildflower honey
1 pound fresh pumpkin, peeled, seeded, & diced in 1-inch cubes	1/4 teaspoon cinnamon
	1/8 teaspoon ground nutmeg
	Crème fraîche
	Toasted pumpkin seeds

Heat ginger and white wine in a medium saucepan over low flame until all of the wine is reduced. Add pumpkin and heavy cream. Slowly simmer until cream has reduced and thickened slightly. Stir in honey, cinnamon, and nutmeg. Transfer soup to a food processor and purée. Adjust seasonings if necessary. Serve hot, topped with a dollop of crème fraîche and sprinkled with toasted pumpkin seeds.

ᚦ Boston Park Plaza Hotel
Boston, Massachusetts

Built in 1927, the Boston Park Plaza Hotel is both elegant and historic. Situated in the heart of Boston, the property has long welcomed its guests with splendid, luxurious accommodations.

The hotel's Cub Club package is one of Boston's best family values. It features first-class, child-proof rooms, over 100 family movies for evening TV entertainment, a story hour complete with milk and cookies, swan boat rides, and a unique coupon book filled with discounts to all major Boston attractions.

The hotel's dining options include Legal Sea Foods, rated one of America's finest, the European and pan-Asian cuisine of Cafe Eurosia, and the bistro-like Café Rouge. For a special treat, guests can indulge in Ben & Jerry's ice cream or enjoy a noontime tea in the Swans Court Lobby Lounge.

☐ *Old-Fashioned Cream of Tomato Soup*

Culinary newsletter editor, Lynn Kerrigan, loves quick, convenient meals made without store-bought convenience foods. Sure, it's easier to open a can of tomato soup, but that wouldn't be as tasty and healthy as Ms. Kerrigan's homemade.

Makes 8 servings.

4 cups tomatoes
1 onion
4 cups water
1 or 2 bouillon cubes
  (optional)

1/2 teaspoon baking soda
2 tablespoons butter
1 tablespoon flour
1 cup milk
Salt, pepper, & herbs to taste

Chop tomatoes into bite-sized pieces. Finely dice onion. Boil tomatoes and onion in 4 cups of water until tomatoes are mushy. For a meaty-tomato flavor, add 1 or 2 bouillon cubes to water before boiling tomatoes. Strain and reserve liquid. Immediately add baking soda to tomato purée. Stir until the foaming stops.

Make a white sauce by cooking butter and flour in a sauce pan, stirring until smooth, slowly adding milk. Cook until white sauce has reached desired consistency. Stir into tomato purée. To thin soup, stir in some of the reserved liquid, if desired. Season to taste with salt, pepper, and herbs.

☯ The Culinary Sleuth
Bryn Mawr, Pennsylvania

The Culinary Sleuth newsletter supplies passionate cooks with unusual culinary information from uncommon sources. The pages of each issue are packed with speciality articles including thrifty home and culinary tips, extra income ideas for home cooks, winning cooking contest hints, where to get free recipes, where to find speciality culinary products, and much more. Published by Page One Cooks publications, the newsletter is an excellent source of practical and valuable culinary tidbits.

☐ *Tomato Consommé*

Guests of The French Room, at The Adolphus, enjoy an elegantly prepared menu of neoclassic cuisine, an exciting step forward in the French culinary tradition. Seasonal selections are prepared by a team of internationally trained chefs, guided by Executive Chef William A. Koval. The cuisine has been described as "masterful" and "angelic." It's rich flavors are achieved through reductions of vegetable stocks and purées, rather than relying extensively on butter and cream.

Serves 8 to 10.

4 cups canned whole tomatoes
4 cups V-8 vegetable juice
4 cups tomato juice
4 cups chicken stock
1/4 cup garlic pearls
1/4 cup fresh basil, chopped
5 skinless chicken breasts,
  ground
10 egg whites
Diced tomatoes for garnish

In a 2-gallon stockpot, combine tomatoes, V-8 juice, tomato juice, chicken stock, garlic, and basil. Simmer for 1-1/2 hours and remove from heat. (Do not blend ingredients.) Pass tomato stock through a medium-grade strainer into a saucepan. Then, pour the tomato stock back into the stockpot and set aside.

Whip ground chicken and egg whites with an electric mixer on slow speed until they are well combined. Stir in tomato stock. Bring to a boil. Reduce to a low heat and simmer for 45 minutes. Pass mixture through cheese cloth. Garnish with diced tomatoes and serve hot.

ୡ The Adolphus
Dallas, Texas

Nationally recognized and critically acclaimed, The French Room has been described by *The New York Times* as "a Louis XV fantasy on the prarie.....indisputably the most striking and sumptuous restaurant in Dallas."

In 1912, St. Louis beer baron Adolphus Busch created The French Room as the crown jewel of his namesake Dallas hotel. It has been faithfully restored to its original grandeur. Among the architectural features of this opulent dining room are murals by Alexander Rosenfield, who also painted the sets for the original production of *Mame* in Philadelphia and the portrait of Laura in the motion picture, *Laura.*

⊓ *Grilled Tomato with Goat Cheese Soup*

Executive Chef Louis Gervais, features daily specialties of light, modern cuisine inspired by the classical cooking of continental Europe such as this Grilled Tomato with Goat Cheese Soup.

Makes 4 servings.

1 pound sliced Roma tomatoes, brushed with olive oil
1 tablespoon garlic
2 tablespoons extra-virgin olive oil
1 potato, peeled & diced
2 cups fresh chicken stock

Pinch sea salt and ground black peppercorn
1/4 cup white wine (Cedar Creek, Pinot Blanc)
8 ounces chèvre (goat cheese)
1 tablespoon mixed fine herbes

Grill tomatoes on barbecue until they have nice markings. In a soup pot, sweat garlic. Add olive oil, diced potatoes, grilled tomatoes, chicken stock, pinch of salt and pepper, and white wine. Simmer until potatoes are tender, then let stand for 30 minutes.

Purée soup. To serve, pour equal amounts soup into each bowl. Garnish with a slice of chèvre and a sprinkle of herbs.

♧ The Sutton Place Hotel
Vancouver, B.C. Canada

The Sutton Place Hotel brings a taste of Europe to one of Canada's most beautiful cities. The hotel is located in the heart of Vancouver, within walking distance of downtown.

Two distinct varieties of dining are available in the hotel's restaurants. Cafe Fleuri offers a full menu of meals featuring North American fare and market specialities that are ever-changing. The Taste of Atlantis, a sumptuous seafood feast, and a decadent 20-item chocolate buffet are among the specials offered in the airy, informal eatery. Le Club has a cozy, more private atmosphere that's conducive to great conversation and fine dining.

The Gerard Lounge is reminiscent of an English club, with tapestries, leather chairs, oil paintings, and cozy fireplace. Voted "best bar" by Vancouver's food critics, the Gerard continues to win accolades for its renown classic martinis.

☐ Roasted Tomato & Turban Squash Soup

Chef Marcus de Konig prepares elegant classic Continental fare in the Deer Path Inn's English Room. The Tea Garden delights diners with it's tranquil setting and an array of colorful flowers and fresh herbs. A variety of English ales can be enjoyed while relaxing in handmade wooden booths in The White Hart Pub.

Yields 6 to 8 servings.

1 large turban squash	4 cups chicken stock
15 plum tomatoes	Chopped chives
3 cloves garlic	4 cups cream
2 red bell peppers	Chopped cilantro and sour
1 large onion, sliced thin	cream for garnish
1/2 cup fresh basil, chopped	

Preheat oven to 350 degrees. Cut squash in half. Remove and discard seeds. Roast squash, whole plum tomatoes, garlic cloves, and bell peppers until tender. Remove skins and/or seeds before setting edible parts aside.

In a stockpot, sauté onions until translucent. Add chopped basil and sauté for 1 minute more. Add chicken stock, squash, tomatoes, garlic, peppers, and chopped chives. Bring to a boil, then reduce heat to a simmer for 15 to 20 minutes. Let cool slightly, then purée in a processor. Run purée through a fine strainer into the pot. Add cream to strained purée. Simmer again until smooth and desired consistency is achieved. Serve in soup bowls garnished with chopped cilantro and sour cream.

⌘ Deer Path Inn
Lake Forest, Illinois

The original Deer Path Inn was built in the 1860s. In 1929 the current inn was completed, duplicating the style of The Manor House (c.1453) located in Chiddingstone, England. The inn's listed in the National Register of Historic Places.

Each of the inn's 62 rooms and suites exhibits traditional English country warmth and charm. The public rooms contain antiques and period furnishings. Leaded windows and the warm fire in the Hearth Room add to the feeling of being nestled away in the English countryside.

☐ *Spicy Vegetable Broth*

This low-fat, chunky vegetable broth, made at Cafe Parizäde, is a favorite of the health-conscious participants of Durham's many diet and fitness centers.

Makes approximately 24 cups.

10 ounces leeks, white & light green part only	8 ounces tomato concasse
1 ounce onions, 1/4-inch dice	Orange zest
8 ounces carrots, 1/4-inch dice	6 ounces corn
8 ounces celery, 1/4-inch dice	8 ounces fennel
6 ounces chilies, 1/4-inch dice	2 bags cleaned spinach chiffonade
Olive oil	Salt & pepper to taste
3 to 4 garlic cloves, minced	Nutmeg (optional)
2 gallons water or stock	Chopped Italian parsley for garnish
Bouquet garni	Giant garlic crouton for garnish
10 ounces cabbage chiffonade	
12 ounces potatoes, 1/4-inch dice	

In a large soup pot, sweat leeks, onions, carrots, celery, and chilies in olive oil. Add garlic and sauté until aroma is evident. Pour in water or stock and spices. Simmer for 15 minutes. Add cabbage and simmer for 10 minutes.

Mix potatoes and continue to simmer for an additional 10 minutes. Add tomato concasse, corn, fennel, and spinach. Season with a hint of salt and pepper. Mix in nutmeg, if desired. Garnish with chopped Italian parsley and a garlic crouton.

⌂ Cafe Parizäde
Durham, North Carolina

Restaurant owner, Giorgio Bakatsias, offers Mediterranean fare in a colorful setting at his location in Erwin Square. The delicious menu samplings include golden Spanish Paella, a Greek country salad, and delicate angel hair pasta with savory sun-dried tomatoes, fresh shrimp, and tangy feta cheese. Regular patrons know to save room for creamy cheesecake or gooey baklava.

The overwhelming success of Cafe Parizäde convinced the restaurateur to expand to accommodate two new ventures: Club Parizäde and Erwin Square Cafe. Club Parizäde caters to private parties as well as regular diners. Erwin Square Cafe serves a variety of imaginative sandwiches and superb salads.

Vegetable Soups

Bean
Soups

🔲 *Black Bean Soup*

Hearty appetites are satisfied after digging into a bowl of inn-keeper Cary Pratt's spicy Black Bean Soup. A dollop of cool yogurt turns down the heat of the salsa. Crisp tortilla chips make perfect dippers.

Makes 10 cups.

2 tablespoons oil	1-1/2 cups chicken broth
1 medium onion, chopped	1 to 2 ounces tequila
4 cloves garlic, minced	3 cups medium chunky salsa
1 tablespoon ground cumin	2 tablespoons fresh lime juice
1 teaspoon crushed red pepper	Yogurt for garnish
32-ounce can black beans	Tortilla chips

Heat oil in a stockpot. Sauté onion, garlic, cumin, and crushed red pepper. Meanwhile, purée black beans with chicken broth and tequila in a food processor. Mix into vegetables. Add salsa and fresh lime juice to stockpot. Bring to a boil then lower heat and simmer for 30 minutes.

Serve hot, topped with a dollop of yogurt. Pass crisp tortilla chips for dipping.

↻ Orinda Bed & Breakfast
Taos, New Mexico

The *Rocky Mountain News* calls the Orinda Bed & Breakfast "a B&B paradise." The updated and enlarged adobe, built in 1949, is surrounded by pasture lands, towering elms, and shimmering cottonwoods. It's a short 15 minute walk into Taos' historic plaza with its many shops, galleries, and restaurants.

The three guest rooms at the inn contain cozy kiva fireplaces, private baths, private entrances, traditional viga-latia ceilings, and wonderful mountain views. The living room holds a guest library and fireplace. A hearty breakfast is served in the main house.

☐ *Calla's Carolina Lima Bean Soup*

Home economist and cooking school owner, Patti Caruana, says chicken bouillon and water can be used in this soup instead of chicken broth. Concentrated ham base and water could also be substituted for the time-consuming process of making broth from a ham bone.

Makes 8 servings.

4 peeled carrots, diced
1 onion, diced
2 stalks celery, diced
3 cloves garlic, diced
5 strips bacon, diced
2 tablespoons shortening
4 cups chicken broth
4 cups ham broth
2 cups chopped fresh tomatoes
  or a 15-ounce can

1 bay leaf
3 tablespoons basil
1 teaspoon thyme
Salt & pepper to taste
1 pound giant lima beans
3 tablespoons Parmesan
  cheese
2-1/2 cups ham chunks (from
  ham bone if available)

Sauté carrots, onion, celery, garlic, and bacon in shortening. Add broths, crushed tomatoes, bay leaf, basil, and thyme. Season with salt and pepper to taste. Add 1 pound giant lima beans. Bring to a boil, reduce heat and simmer until beans are tender, approximately 1-1/2 to 2 hours.

Before serving, add Parmesan cheese and ham chunks.

♧ Calla's cooking school
Baldwinsville, New York

Patti Caruana, chef instructor for Calla's, mixes all the right ingredients to teach small, informal cooking classes. She expertly conducts basic to advanced cooking classes for singles, couples, newlyweds, seniors, and organizations. In addition to teaching, Caruana is the operator of As You Like It Catering.

☐ *Dixieland Delight's Pinto Beans*

Paris Permenter and John Bigley, authors of the book Texas Barbecue, *received this recipe from the Dixieland Delights, a team of barbecue competitors who say there's one secret to making good beans, "Put 'em in and let 'em go."*

Serves 12.

1 pound pinto beans	Pinch cayenne pepper
2 cans Rotel diced tomatoes and chiles	Sprinkle of basil
3 shakes salt	2 shakes black pepper
Sprinkle of ground cumin	3 sliced jalapeño peppers
1/2 teaspoon hot chili powder	1/2 pound bacon
Pinch of paprika	1-1015 (a sweet Texas onion) or a white onion, diced

Rinse beans and soak overnight covered in water. Drain beans, rinse well and transfer to a large pot. Add all remaining ingredients and cover with fresh water. Cover pot and cook on a firebox for about 6 hours or on a stove 5 to 6 hours. If you cook on the stove, stir more frequently to keep the beans from sticking.

♧ Texas Barbecue

In the Lone Star State, soup is often as substantial as a pot of pintos, wickedly spiced with tomatoes and chilies. The award-winning book, *Texas Barbecue* is a look at the best pits, products, and prize-winning recipes in Texas. There are recipes for smoking, grilling, or cooking almost anything in the smoker from meats, seafood, vegetables, beans, and suggestions for side dishes and desserts including cobblers, banana pudding, and pecan pie.

⊓ White Bean Soup with Vegetables & Basil

This Ojai Valley Inn soup is light, tasty, and healthy. It's also easy to make.

Makes approximately 16 servings.

1 pound cannellini beans
3 tablespoons olive oil
1 pound domestic mushrooms
4 large carrots, peeled & diced medium
3 large yellow onions, diced medium
2 leeks, white part & a little of pale green part, thoroughly washed, diced medium
10 Roma tomatoes, diced medium
2 bay leaves
1 gallon chicken stock
Salt & pepper to taste
Basil Purée (recipe follows)
Baguette Croutons (recipe follows)

Soak beans in water overnight. The next day cook beans until tender. Strain and layout on a sheet pan to cool.

While beans are cooking, heat olive oil in a large soup pot over high heat until very hot. Cut mushrooms into quarters, add to pot, and cook, stirring occasionally for 3 minutes. Add carrots, onions, leeks, Roma tomatoes, and bay leaves. Cook for 6 to 7 minutes. Pour in stock and simmer for 30 minutes. Add cooked beans. Salt and pepper to taste.

To serve, ladle soup into individual bowls. Drizzle with 3/4 tablespoon of Basil Purée. Garnish with a Baguette Crouton.

Basil Purée

1 cup fresh basil leaves
1/2 cup extra virgin olive oil
1 teaspoon salt

Place all ingredients in a blender and blend well.

Baguette Croutons

1 baguette, sliced on the bias into 1/4-inch slices
Extra-virgin olive oil
Salt

Brush baguette with extra-virgin olive oil and season with a little salt. Grill the bread or toast in the oven.

Ojai Valley Inn
Ojai, California

The elegant Ojai Valley Inn is recognized as one of California's finest historic resorts. Set in a stimulating, yet peaceful environment, the inn's a leisurely drive from the hustle and bustle of city life. Amenities include 212 deluxe rooms, casual and formal dining, 18-hole golf course, tennis courts, swimming, horseback riding, exercise facility, and a children's playground.

For breakfast, a romantic dinner, or an incredible weekend brunch, dining at the Ojai Valley Inn features a wide variety of cuisine choices. Several restaurants provide settings overlooking panoramic mountain views, pools, and the resort's well-known golf course.

Bean Soups

⬜ *Roasted Onion Soup with Cannellini Beans*

Sundance resort's Executive Chef, Don Heidel, created this recipe which originally served 50 and has now been adapted for home cooking. Cannellini beans are white kidney beans, a staple in Italian kitchens.

Makes 10 servings.

1 pound onions, roasted & julienne
9-2/3 cups chicken stock
6-1/3 ounces cannellini beans, cooked
1/3 ounce Balsamic vinegar

1/4 ounce basil, julienne
3-1/4 tablespoons Parmesan cheese, grated
Salt & pepper to taste

In a large stockpot, combine all ingredients. Simmer until thoroughly heated and flavors are well combined.

Each serving contains only 39 calories and 1 gram of fat.

⌇ Sundance Resort
Sundance, Utah

Country Living magazine finds, "The architecture at Sundance -- like its cuisine -- is straightforward and unpretentious." The Tree Room, graced by Native American art and Western memorabilia from Robert Redford's personal collection, offers elegant dining by candlelight or outdoor dining in the Tree Room Garden. The Grill Room is a relaxed and informal gathering place set amongst a photographic history of the Sundance Institute.

Zoom Roadhouse Grill, housed in a large Victorian frame structure that was once the Union Pacific Railway Depot in Park City, has an ambiance that is warm, comfortable, informal, and enjoyable. The atmosphere is as relaxed as eating soup and sandwiches at the kitchen table. Zoom offers the casual vibrance of a roadhouse eatery without the noise and bright lights of a diner.

☐ *Mixed Bean Soup*

A steaming bowl of bean soup is an ideal meal-in-one. Ounce for ounce, the humble bean costs less and provides more nutrients than most other foods. It's also tops in versatility as you can change the flavor of each potful with the addition of a variety of meats, grains, or vegetables. Soup's On! coauthor, Gail Hobbs, often omits the ham and adds a cup or two of cooked brown rice to her bean soup.

Makes 12 servings.

1 pound dry bean & barley mix
2 tablespoons olive oil
1 cup chopped onion
1 cup chopped carrots
1/2 cup *each* chopped red & green bell peppers
1 tablespoon minced garlic

8 cups vegetable or chicken broth
1 pound lean cooked ham, chopped
1/4 cup Worcestershire sauce
Salt and black pepper to taste

Place dry bean mix in a large stockpot and cover (plus 2 or 3 inches) with cold water. Cover and bring to a rolling boil for 2 minutes. Remove from heat and soak, covered, for about 1-1/2 hours. Then, drain beans, sort, rinse, and set aside.

In the same stockpot, heat olive oil. Sauté chopped onions, carrots, peppers, and garlic over medium-high heat for about 10 minutes until softened. Add bean mix, broth, and ham. Simmer, covered, for 2 to 3 hours, stirring occasionally, until beans are soft.

Stir in Worcestershire sauce and season to taste with salt and pepper. Serve hot immediately or freeze in airtight containers.

Don't be tempted to add the Worcestershire sauce (or any other acidic food like tomatoes) to the soup before it is finished cooking. The beans won't soften completely if you do.

⬜ *Savory Split Pea Soup*

This recipe is so simple to make and simply delicious. Culinary newsletter editor, Marilyn Helton, advises, "If you're not too fond of oregano, try the mildly-flavored Greek variety."

Makes 8 servings.

2 cups lean ham, cubed or 1
  meaty ham bone
1 pound split peas, rinsed
2 large onions, chopped
3 stalks celery, chopped
3 carrots, finely sliced or
  chopped

2 cloves garlic, minced
1 bay leaf
1/2 teaspoon oregano
1 teaspoon dry mustard
8 cups cold water

Place all ingredients in a large soup pot. Bring to a boil then, reduce heat. Cover and simmer for 2 hours, stirring occasionally. Remove the ham bone, if using one, take off meat and cut in pieces and add back to soup.

This soup can either be thinned with water or thickened by boiling away liquid with the lid off.

⊄⊃ Cinnamon Hearts
Modesto, California

Cinnamon Hearts is a beautifully prepared, thoughtfully written, and tastefully presented culinary newsletter with full-color Victorian-style prints. It's creator, Marilyn Helton, puts her heart and soul into each exquisite issue and gives her readers healthy recipes to make and savor while celebrating the joy of life.

Regular columns and special features include articles with recipes such as "Taking Time Out," "Once Upon A Recipe," "From The Country Cupboard," Bob Carter's "Traveling à la Carter," and "How Does Your Garden Grow?"

Very Good
Dec 116

🗋 *Lentil Soup*

The owner of Granby House Bed and Breakfast, Pauline Lacroix, receives many requests for her favorite Lentil Soup recipe. Here it is just for you.

Makes approximately 10 to 12 servings.

2 cups of lentils	1/2 teaspoon thyme
8 cups cold water	1 bay leaf
1/2 pound ham bone	2 tablespoons butter
1 cup chopped celery	2 tablespoons flour
2 large carrots, chopped	Juice of 1 lemon
28-ounce can chopped Italian	1 tablespoon salt
tomatoes with liquid	Freshly ground pepper
3 potatoes, peeled & cubed	1/2 cup parsley, chopped
1 cup chopped onions	Lemon slices for garnish

Soak lentils in cold water for 3 hours. Drain and place in a large soup pot with 2 quarts of water. Add ham bone. Cover and simmer, skimming lightly. Cook slowly for 2 to 3 hours.

Add chopped vegetables, thyme, and bay leaf. Cover and simmer for 30 minutes. Add more liquid if necessary. Remove bay leaf and bone. Shred any lean meat off the bone and return to pot.

In a separate sauce pan, melt butter and blend in flour. Stir carefully into soup. Simmer for 10 minutes. Add lemon juice, salt, and pepper. Garnish individual bowls with parsley and lemon slices.

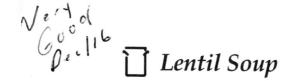

Granby House Bed and Breakfast
Toronto, Canada

Visitors to Toronto have a charming and beautiful lodging alternative. The Granby House is situated in the heart of downtown and is a short stroll to shopping, theatres, galleries, restaurants, and cafes. Additionally, the bed and breakfast is close to Ontario Place, Harbourfront, Yorkville, Maple Leaf Gardens, and the Canadian National Tower.

Bean Soups

Meat
Soups

⬜ *Beef Vegetable Soup*

Here's a comforting, down-home soup from a Southern restaurant rated four stars in the Mobile Travel Guide.

Makes 6 to 8 servings.

3/4 pound cubed lean beef
16-ounce can whole tomatoes
3 large onions, quartered
3 or 4 carrots, peeled & sliced
1 teaspoon sweet basil
2 cups sliced celery

16-ounce package frozen
 gumbo blend (cut okra &
 whole kernel corn)
1 cup uncooked noodles
Seasonings to taste

Cover meat with hot water. Add tomatoes and onions. Cook over low heat until meat is tender, about 2 to 2-1/2 hours. Add remaining ingredients, except for noodles, and cook for another 30 to 45 minutes over low heat. Stir in noodles and cook for 15 minutes more. Season to taste.

⌂ Walnut Hills
Vicksburg, Mississippi

Good ol' Southern cooking is the speciality of the Walnut Hills restaurant located in historic Vicksburg. The menu features country favorites including fried corn, country fried steak, purple hull peas, mustard greens, creamed potatoes, and blackberry cobbler for dessert. Like many great country feasts, in addition to soup and salad, there's a choice of biscuits or cornbread.

Beef Soups

⊓ *Great Basin Vegetable*
Soup with Braised Beef

Chef Don Heidel's soup is an example of honest American cooking with pure, high-quality ingredients. Robert Redford's Sundance Resort is well on its way to becoming 100% self-sufficient with its expansive organic garden providing an abundance of vegetables grown from heritage seeds, the ones Americans grew generations ago, before hybrids were invented.

Serves 10 (originally served 50.)

2 pounds beef shanks
8 cups white beef stock
1-1/4 ounces olive oil
3/4 leek, sliced thin
1/3 yellow onion, diced
   medium
1-1/4 carrots, diced small
1/4 bunch celery, diced
   medium
3/4 turnip, diced medium

1/8 head green cabbage,
   chiffonade
3/4 cup corn
1/3 tomato concasse
1-1/4 garlic cloves, minced
2-1/3 teaspoons mixed herbs
1-1/4 teaspoons hickory spice
1-1/4 potatoes, diced medium
1/3 cup chestnut lima beans
Salt & pepper to taste

Grill beef shanks, then cover with stock and braise until tender. Heat oil in a large stockpot. Add leek, onion, carrot, celery, turnip, cabbage, corn, tomato, and garlic. Sauté until tender. Mix in herbs and hickory spice and simmer. Add stock and potatoes and simmer until potatoes are done. Cook lima beans separately, then add to soup. Remove meat from shanks and dice. Return to soup. Season with salt and pepper.

☐ *Herb Vegetable Beef Soup*

This full-bodied soup was created by food and wine authority Shirley Sarvis especially to serve with Sanford Winery's 1991 Pinot Noir Vin Gris. If you'd like to add a little different variation to the soup, add 1 or 2 thinly sliced artichoke hearts during the last 30 minutes of cooking.

Makes 4 main-course servings.

3/4 pound lean ground round beef
1 cup finely chopped onions
1/3 cup Sanford Pinot Noir Vin Gris
1/2 teaspoon finely chopped needles of fresh rosemary (or about 1/2 teaspoon crumbled dried rosemary)
1/2 teaspoon crumbled dried thyme

1 large can (1 pound, 12 ounces) peeled whole tomatoes, broken up
3 cups mild, lean beef broth
1-1/2 cups peeled carrots, sliced diagonally 3/16-inch thick
1-1/2 cups celery, sliced diagonally
Salt to taste

In a large heavy kettle over medium heat, cook beef until crumbly and lightly browned. Add onions and cook until limp. Stir in wine and cook until it evaporates. Mix in rosemary, thyme, tomatoes, broth, carrots, and celery. Sprinkle with approximately 1/4 teaspoon salt. Stir to combine, cover, and simmer slowly for 1-1/2 to 3 hours.

Season to taste with salt. Garnish each serving with a small sprig of fresh rosemary, if desired.

℃ Sanford Winery & Ranch
Buellton, California

Sanford Winery and vineyards are located in the rolling hills of Santa Ynez Valley. The winery's annual production is 30,000 cases. Current varieties include Chardonnay, Sauvignon Blanc, Pinot Noir, and Pinot Noir-Vin Gris, a barrel-fermented Blanc de Noir wine.

Owners Richard and Thekla Sanford and their knowledgable staff welcome visitors to the winery's tasting and sales facility daily where a picnic area is available for relaxing, sipping, and feasting.

🍲 *Pork and Apple Chowder*

This recipe by Chef Mike Matteo is great with fresh baked bread on a chilly fall evening.

Makes 12 servings.

2 ounces salted butter
1 pound trimmed, boneless
  pork, cut in 1-inch cubes
6 ounces Spanish onion,
  1/2-inch dice
6 ounces celery, 1/2-inch slices
23 ounces apple juice
1-1/2 quarts chicken stock

1 pound red beet (baby new)
  potatoes, diced
1 pound fresh apples (Granny
  Smith or other), diced
1/2 teaspoon nutmeg
1/2 teaspoon cinnamon
1-1/2 teaspoons salt
2 teaspoons pepper

In a heavy sauce pot, melt salted butter. Add pork and cook until brown. Add diced onions and sliced celery. Sauté until the vegetables are clear. Over medium heat, add apple juice and chicken stock. Bring to a boil and simmer for 45 minutes. Add potatoes and continue to simmer for 1/2 an hour. Add apples and spices. Cook until apples are just softened. Serve hot.

🍴 Chef Mike Matteo
Rochester, New York

Chef Matteo is a 22-year veteran of the hospitality industry. He's a graduate of the Rochester Institute of Technology School of Food, Hotel, and Tourism.

His culinary talents are varied. He has taught cooking for many years and recently produced a week-long cooking class for children. During the class, children ages 8-12 created their own recipes and produced their own cookbooks. Chef Mike is currently at work on his own cookbook for children.

Chef Mike's Catering produces weddings, receptions, ice sculptures, and cooking demonstrations for celebrities such as Jack Nicklaus and Don McLean.

☐ Grilled Corn Tortilla Soup with Gingered Pork Potstickers

Chef John Bobrick's inspirational regional cuisine served at the Inn of the Anasazi, in historic downtown Santa Fe, New Mexico, has earned the Anasazi Restaurant many awards including a four-diamond from the Automobile Association of America..

Makes approximately 8 servings.

1/2 cup olive oil
3 jalapeño peppers, half with seeds
10 cloves garlic
9 cups corn tortilla strips
2 yellow onions, sliced
8 ounces Sacramento tomato juice (or any other brand)

8 cups chicken stock
1 tablespoon tomato paste
2 tablespoons cumin
1 tablespoon chopped cilantro
Salt & pepper to taste
Gingered Pork Potstickers (recipe follows)

In a large stockpot, heat oil until smoking. Fry jalapeños, garlic, and tortilla strips until crispy. Remove 1/2 cup of the tortilla strips and reserve for garnish. Add onions and sauté for 2 minutes. Deglaze with tomato juice and chicken stock. Boil for 10 minutes. Add tomato paste, cumin, and cilantro. Season to taste with salt and pepper. Purée in food processor until smooth. Place broth in bowls. Top with 1/2 cup of the reserved tortilla strips and 2 potstickers.

Gingered Pork Potstickers

1/2 pound ground pork
1 tablespoon ginger, minced
1 tablespoon garlic, minced
2 tablespoons soy sauce
1 tablespoon sesame sauce
1 tablespoon chili flakes

1 bunch green onions, sliced
1 bunch parsley, sliced
1 bunch cilantro, chopped
3 eggs
Salt & pepper as desired
1 package wonton skins

Combine all ingredients except wonton skins. Place small amount of mixture in skins and form to shape. Steam in a double boiler until wonton skins are tender and pork is cooked through.

☐ *Orchid's Minnesota Wild Rice Soup*

Kentucky ham is dry-cured like Virginia ham. It's quite salty so don't be tempted to add salt to this soup until it's finished cooking and you've tasted it.

Makes 8 -- 6 ounce servings.

8 ounces butter	1 teaspoon shallots
12 ounces raw wild rice	2 ounces carrots
16 ounces chicken stock	4 ounces Kentucky ham
2 ounces celery	8 ounces heavy cream
2 ounces onions	8 ounces veal stock

Heat 4 ounces of the butter in a saucepan. Add raw wild rice and stir to coat with butter. Add chicken stock. Bring to a boil and simmer until liquid is absorbed and rice is cooked. Set aside.

Chop vegetables and ham. In another large stockpot, heat the remaining 4 ounces of butter. Add celery, onions, shallots, carrots, and Kentucky ham. Sauté for 3 minutes or until vegetables become transparent. Add heavy cream and veal stock. Bring to a boil and reduce to desired consistency. Add wild rice and simmer for an additional 5 minutes.

⌇ Omni Netherland Plaza
Cincinnati, Ohio

The Omni Netherland Plaza offers three gracious dining experiences. Orchids, for elegant dining, Cafe at the Palm Court, for light fare, and Palm Court Bar & Hors d'Oeuvrie, for refreshments and entertainment.

Executive Chef Damian Reolon has been associated with the Omni for more than a decade. He has performed culinary magic for hotels in Switzerland, France, Sweden, Greece, Italy, Hong Kong, Malaysia, and Hawaii. His world-renowned cuisines have been served to kings, queens, princes, and U.S. Presidents.

⬜ Smoked Ham Hock and Mustard Green Soup with White Beans, Roasted Tomatoes and Thyme

Executive Chef Brent Wertz delights the Mohonk Mountain House guests with a unique American food experience. This is one of his finest soups.

Makes 15 portions.

6 cloves roasted garlic
1 bunch thyme, minced
2 ounces olive oil
8 ounces Chardonnay wine
1/2 gallon well-flavored
   smoked ham hock stock
2 pounds white beans, soaked
   & cooked in ham hock stock

4 pints cherry tomatoes,
   roasted light brown
Salt & pepper to taste
Honeyed Mustard Greens
   (recipe follows)
Sweet basil, chiffonade for
   garnish

Chop roasted garlic and sauté with thyme in olive oil in a large pot. Deglaze with wine. Add stock, white beans, and roasted tomatoes. Simmer for 45 minutes. Season to taste with salt and pepper. To serve, Place soup in bowl with 2 roasted tomatoes. Garnish with Honeyed Mustard Greens and basil.

Honeyed Mustard Greens

1 pound mustard greens
1 ounce whole butter
2 ounces shallots

3 tablespoons honey
1/2 teaspoon roasted caraway
Salt & pepper to taste

Blanch mustard greens slightly. Drain. Place greens, butter, and shallots in a sauté pan. Cook over low heat for 2 to 3 minutes. Add honey, caraway seeds, and salt and pepper to taste.

Pork Soups

☐ *Pea Soup with Ham & Cheese Dumplings*

Healthy Exchanges *creator, JoAnna Lund, maintains her 130 pound weight loss with low-fat soups like this one .*

Serves 6.

2 cups (16-ounce can) peas, rinsed & drained
1-1/2 cups plus 2 tablespoons water
2 cups (16-ounce can) Healthy Request Chicken Broth
1/8 teaspoon black pepper
1 cup (5 ounces) diced raw potato
3/4 cup shredded carrot
1/4 cup finely chopped onion

1/2 cup (3 ounces) finely diced Dubuque 97% Fat Free Ham or any other extra-lean ham
6 tablespoons Bisquick Reduced Fat Baking Mix
1 teaspoon dried parsley flakes
1/4 cup skim milk
3 tablespoons (3/4 ounce) shredded Kraft Reduced Fat Cheddar Cheese

Place peas with 2 tablespoons of water in a blender container. Cover and purée for 30 seconds. In a large saucepan, combine pea purée, remaining 1-1/2 cups water, chicken broth, and pepper. Add potatoes, carrots, and onion. Mix well to combine and bring mixture to a boil. Lower heat. Cover. Simmer 15 minutes.

In a medium bowl, combine ham, baking mix, parsley, skim milk, and cheese. Add into hot mixture to form 6 dumplings. Cover and continue cooking 10 minutes or until dumplings are firm. For each serving, place 1 dumpling into a bowl and spoon about 1 cup soup over top. Serve at once.

⚘ Healthy Exchanges
DeWitt, Iowa

Housewife JoAnna Lund's love of food created a serious weight problem. After trying and failing many diets to lose weight, she slammed the refrigerator door shut. She then devised a method of exchanges to enable her to eat all the foods she loved by exchanging fats and sugars for healthier choices. By reducing her caloric intake, the pounds dropped off, and she published her collection of "common folk" recipes in a cookbook. The word of Lund's success spread and the demand for her recipes increased. She now publishes a monthly food newsletter, cookbooklets, and writes cookbooks published by G.P. Putnam.

Pork Soups

☐ *Lamb Soup*

Chef Mark Dayanandan learned early in life how to prepare a wonderful meal using basic, fresh ingredients. He's an avid cookbook reader who doesn't like to use the so-called "convenience products." Lamb Soup is one of his fabulous " from scratch" dishes.

Yields 6 portions.

1 pound diced lamb shoulder	3 cloves garlic, chopped
3 tablespoons olive oil	10 ounces plum tomatoes,
1 tablespoon flat leaf parsley	peeled & chopped
1 small onion, diced	8 cups white veal stock
1 medium carrot, diced	Seasoning to taste
2 stalks celery, diced	Thick crouton for garnish

In a deep saucepan, sauté diced lamb in olive oil until well browned. Add parsley, onions, carrots, celery, and garlic and continue cooking for several minutes. Next, put in the tomatoes and stock and bring to a boil. Let simmer for approximately 1 hour. Skim the surface of the soup, adjust seasoning, and serve over a thick crouton.

⌂ Marriott's Bay Point Resort
Panama City Beach, Florida

From Fiddler's Green to Tucker's, Marriott's Bay Point Resort's restaurants and lounges cater to discriminating palates and slim or bulging pocketbooks. Included in the wide array of feasting options are Fiddler's Green, the resorts fine-dining focal point, Circes, a sports bar with big screen TV's and nightly entertainment, Teddy's Back Bay Beach Club, an unpretentious, open-air eatery perched on the end of a 385-yard-long boardwalk, and the poolside Bay Breeze Bar.

Chef Dayanandan's extensive culinary experience and fine touch influences the food preparation and presentation at the Marriott. "It takes finesse to showcase an entrée so it doesn't look manhandled," he says. "We tweak each serving so it has color and eye-appeal."

☐ *Lamb Orzo Soup*

The Peabody chefs serve global-American cuisine, taking the freshest vegetables and finest ingredients available and melding them with an interesting blend of flavors and spices. Lamb Orzo Soup is an example of their talents.

Yields 10 cups.

2 tablespoons garlic, sliced
2 tablespoons olive oil
1-1/2 pounds leg of lamb, trimmed & diced 1/4-inch
1 cup white wine
5 cups lamb stock
1 cup tomato concasse
1 teaspoon fresh oregano

Salt & pepper to taste
Garnish ingredients: 2 cups julienne onions, 2 teaspoons olive oil, & 1/4 teaspoon cinnamon
1 cup orzo (rice-shaped pasta), cooked

In a heavy pan, sauté garlic in olive oil until light brown. Add lamb and sauté until light brown. Stir in wine and simmer to reduce by half. Pour in lamb stock and simmer for 20 minutes. Add tomato and oregano. Simmer for 5 minutes. Season with salt and pepper to taste.

To prepare garnish, sauté onions in olive oil until light brown. Add cinnamon, then season to taste with salt and pepper. Place cooked orzo on soup first and top with onion mixture.

⟐ The Peabody Orlando
Orlando, Florida

The now-famous March of The Peabody Ducks takes place daily at 11 a.m. and 5 p.m. in the Lobby of the Peabody Orlando hotel. It has to be seen to be believed.

This 891-room hotel offers many personalized services that makes each guest feel as comfortable as possible while they're traveling. The B-Line Diner, an authentic fifties-style diner, is open 24-hours a day and serves pure American food with California highlights. The vibrant eatery features daily "blue plate" specials and delectable pastries and desserts prepared daily in the on-site pastry shop. Guests on the go can take advantage of the B-Line Express window offering carry-out dining at its finest.

☐ *Scotch Broth*

This old Scottish soup is from the cookbook Auld Favorites -- Recipes from the Members and Friends of the Scottish Society of the Pikes Peak Region. *Mutton is the meat of a mature sheep, as distinguished from the younger lamb.*

Makes 6 servings.

1 pound neck of mutton
8 cups cold water
1 teaspoon salt
2 tablespoons *each* pearl
  barley, yellow split peas,
  & dried green peas
3 medium carrots, chopped

2 leeks, well washed, chopped
3 tablespoons turnip, diced
1 medium onion, chopped
1/2 small cabbage, chopped
1 teaspoon finely chopped
  parsley
Salt & pepper to taste

Put meat, water, salt, barley, yellow peas, and green peas into a large stockpot. Bring to a boil, very slowly. Skim as needed. Add remaining vegetables and return to a boil. Gently simmer until meat is cooked and vegetables are tender, about 2 hours. Add parsley. Season with salt and pepper to taste.

ᓚ Pikes Peak Highland Games and Celtic Festival
Colorado Springs, Colorado

The dynamic Pikes Peak Highland Games and Celtic Festival is held annually on the third Saturday of July. The one-day event is one of the special ways the Society shares its Scottish heritage with the entire community of Colorado Springs. It's open to the general public and features all manners of things Scottish, including vendor's wares. Highland dancers, pipe majors, bagpipe bands, and a large number of individual pipers and drummers take part in a lively competition. Scottish heavy athletes, both men and women, compete with fierce determination at tossing cabers, sheafs, and stones. Young tykes take part in youthful games throughout the day's festivities.

Lamb Soups

⬚ *Sausage Lentil Fricot*

Never one to be totally satisfied with a soup recipe, Shirley Hollink, remarks "This is a recipe which has evolved, and I continue to experiment with other ingredients as fresh vegetables come into season."

Makes approximately 6 servings.

1/2 pound bulk Italian sausage	4 cups canned low-salt
1 large onion, finely chopped	chicken broth
1 large clove garlic, minced	1 bay leaf
1 bunch green Swiss chard,	3/4 cup lentils
washed & diced	2 cups water
1 small carrot, shredded	1/2 cup egg flake pasta
28-ounce can whole tomatoes	1/4 cup Dijon mustard
in juice, coarsely chopped	Splash lemon juice

In a frying pan, brown sausage, remove and crumble. Sauté onion and garlic until crisp tender. Put sausage, onion, and garlic in a large soup pot. Add Swiss chard, carrot, tomatoes, chicken broth, bay leaf, lentils, water, and pasta. Cover and simmer for 1 hour or until ingredients are tender. Add Dijon mustard and splash of lemon juice. Remove bay leaf and enjoy with crusty bread.

⌂ Sandy Creek Manor House
Hamlin, New York

Shirley Hollink welcomes guests to the Sandy Creek Manor House, but it's Paradise, the cat, who's considered queen of the house. Perhaps that's one reason pets are always welcome to visit this quiet and comfortable European-style bed and breakfast.

Visitors to the Manor marvel at the glorious works of Mother Nature while strolling around 6 wooded acres, experience the thrill of salmon fishing, and reminisce of days gone by when listening to the antique player piano. According to Shirley, "All guest rooms offer the warmth of Amish quilts and feather pillows ... and breakfast is prepared with love."

Garlic & Lentil Soup with Duck Breast

Chef Alain Borel creates elegant cuisine carefully seasoned and with a light hand on the sauces. Each dish is picture-perfect, designed to please the eye as well as the palate.

Makes approximately 8 servings.

2 tablespoons olive oil
1 cup chopped garlic, about 4 heads
1/4 cup shallots, chopped
2 medium carrots, finely chopped
1/2 cup flour
2 cups Côtes du Rhône or other hearty red wine
1 gallon duck stock
2 bay leaves
3 sprigs sage, chopped
1-1/2 cups lentils
Salt & pepper to taste
2 cooked duck breasts
1 tomato, diced, at room temperature

Place olive oil, garlic, shallots, and carrots in a large cooking pot. Cook on medium heat for 2 minutes or until vegetables sweat but do not brown. Add flour and mix well. Pour in red wine and stir well to incorporate. Add duck stock, bay leaves, sage, and lentils. Bring to a boil, then reduce heat to a simmer. Continue cooking until liquid is reduced by 1/4 and lentils are tender.

Salt and pepper to taste. Just before serving, slice duck breast and julienne. Place strips of duck breast in bottom of individual soup bowls. Ladle a generous serving of soup over duck breast. Garnish with diced tomato. Serve hot.

L'Auberge Provencal
White Post, Virginia

Guests of L'Auberge Provencale discover the feeling of a real country inn of the South of France. Innkeepers Alain and Celeste Borel pride themselves in providing truly romantic accommodations and widely acclaimed French cuisine.

Fine hospitality is the keystone of the inn. The 10 guest rooms are tastefully decorated with Victorian and European furnishings and antiques. Evening meals are offered at the Manor House, Mt. Airy (circa 1753) in one of three intimate dining rooms. In the morning, guests are offered a multi-course gourmet breakfast feast.

Duck Soups

Poultry
Soups

⊓ *Mrs. C's Chicken Chardonnay Soup*

The secret of Mrs. C's magical soup is the use of fresh ingredients, Casa Larga Chardonnay, and most importantly, a whole lot of love.

Makes enough to revitalize a group of weary grape pickers.

1 whole stewing chicken, cut up or 4 breasts of chicken
1/3 cup apple vinegar
2 tablespoons plus a few pinches salt
4 celery stalks, cleaned
4 carrots, cleaned & peeled
3 onions, sliced

4 fresh cleaned tomatoes, cut up or 4 peeled canned Italian plum tomatoes
1 head escarole, cleaned & cut
1/2 cup fresh Italian parsley
1 garlic clove, chopped
1/2 bottle (375 ml) Casa Larga Reserve Chardonnay

Soak chicken parts in cold water with apple vinegar and 1 tablespoon of the salt for about 1/2 an hour. Meanwhile, fill an 8-quart cooking pot with cold water and the remaining 1 tablespoon of the salt and bring to a boil. Rinse soaking chicken and add to cooking pot. Boil for approximately 10 minutes. Remove pot from heat, take out chicken and set aside. Empty water from pot, wash, and refill with clean water. Bring to a boil, add chicken and all vegetables. Simmer for 20 minutes.

Remove chicken, rinse under cold water, remove skin and bones. Rinse chicken again and return to pot of boiling water. Cook for about 1 hour, skimming foam as necessary. Soup is done when carrots and celery are soft. Stir in Chardonnay wine and simmer for an additional 10 minutes. Strain soup into another large pot. Serve chicken bouillon steaming hot.

⊊ Casa Larga Vineyards
Fairport, New York

A visit to Casa Larga Vineyards provides a chance to tour the winery and see where grapes are grown, harvested, crushed, pressed, and aged. Tasting opportunities occur in the Private Tasting Room, complete with Italian marble, vaulted ceilings, and vineyard views. Picnic facilities are the perfect spot to relax, enjoy fine wine, and savor the beauty of upstate New York.

⊔ *Poblano & Smoked Chicken Chowder with Hominy*

This hearty, unusual soup is from John Ash's cookbook, From the Earth to the Table: John Ash's Wine Country Cuisine, *published by Dutton in 1995. Ash explains about the recipe, "The smoky flavor of the poblano chile is even better if you char-roast it before adding it in. If poblanos aren't available, Anaheim chiles can substitute nicely. If nei-ther are available, regular green bell peppers, which have been char-roasted and peeled, will work, but you'll need to add a little chile powder to approximate the zing of the poblanos."*

Serves 6 to 8.

2 tablespoons olive oil
1 pound yellow onions, halved & sliced lengthwise
3 medium poblano chiles, seeded & sliced into thin strips
1 tablespoon finely slivered garlic
2 cups husked & quartered tomatillos (small, green tomato with a paper-like brown covering)
1/2 teaspoon fennel seed
1/2 teaspoon cumin seed
2 teaspoons dried oregano (Mexican preferred)
1/4 teaspoon cinnamon

1-1/2 cups seeded & diced tomatoes (drain if using canned)
6 cups rich chicken stock
2 cups fruity white wine, such as Gewürztraminer or Riesling
1/2 pound smoked chicken, julienned
3/4 cup canned, drained white hominy
Kosher salt & freshly ground black pepper
For garnish: chopped fresh cilantro, diced avocado, & fresh lime juice

In a saucepan, heat the olive oil. Add the onions, poblanos, and garlic. Sauté until soft but not brown, about 5 minutes. Add tomatillos, fennel seed, cumin seed, oregano, cinnamon, tomatoes, chicken stock, and wine. Simmer gently for 15 minutes. Add the smoked chicken and hominy. Simmer to heat through. Season to taste with salt and pepper.

Garnish with chopped cilantro, diced avocado, and lime juice just before serving.

Recommended wine: The tart flavors of the tomatillos and fruity stock are augmented by a similarly fruity Johannisberg Riesling or Gewürztraminer.

⑈ Chef John Ash
Sonoma County, California

John Ash serves as the Culinary Director of the Valley Oaks Food and Wine Center at Fetzer Vineyards. It's here that Ash cooks daily from the bounty of a five-acre organic garden. He chooses from more than 1000 varieties of fruits, vegetables, herbs, and edible flowers. Chef Ash ran his own successful restaurant, John Ash & Co., in Santa Rosa during the 1980s.

His cookbook, *From the Earth to the Table: John Ash's Wine Country Cuisine* won the 1996 "Best Cookbook of the Year" award given by the International Association of Cooking Professionals. The book focuses on utilizing fresh, organic, locally-grown ingredients and pairing each dish with a complementary wine. Ash's 25 years of experience in creating naturally low-fat, high-flavor meals is evident in the book's more than 300 recipes for salads, soups, pastas, pizzas, risottos, fish, poultry, meats, breads, beverages, and desserts.

Chicken Soups

☐ *Cures Anything Chicken Soup*

According to Soup's On! coauthor, Bob Carter, "I'm no doctor but this soup, once served to me on a sick bed, is said to be recommended for poor health, bad disposition, unsavory character, all loved ones, hot weather, cold weather, staying home, family outings, summer, winter, spring, autumn, and just for the heck of it."

Makes 6 servings.

5 cups chicken broth
1 cup water
1/4 cup long grain rice
1/3 cup lemon juice
3 large eggs

1/2 pound skinless, boneless
chicken breast, cut into
1/4-inch pieces
Salt & pepper to taste
2 tablespoons fresh dill

In a saucepan, combine broth and water. Bring to a boil. Stir in rice and simmer, covered, for 15 minutes, or until tender. In a bowl, whisk together 1/4 cup of the lemon juice and eggs. Whisk in 1 cup of the hot broth. Whisk that mixture into the remaining broth. Add chicken, and cook over moderate heat, whisking for 3 minutes or until chicken is cooked and soup is slightly thickened. Add salt and pepper to taste, and remaining lemon juice. Serve soup sprinkled with snipped fresh dill.

☐ *Coconut Curry Chicken Soup*

Chef Patrick Fobert's Coconut Curry Chicken Soup was an award winner at the 1995 St. Kitt's/Nevis culinary competition.

Makes 6 to 8 servings.

1 tablespoon vegetable oil
2 boneless, skinless chicken breasts, diced
2 tablespoons curry powder
4 ounces onion, diced
4 ounces carrot, diced
4 ounces celery, diced
4 ounces potato, diced
1 teaspoon ginger, chopped
3 pegs garlic, chopped
1 teaspoon lemon grass, chopped

1 can unsweetened coconut milk
4 cups chicken or vegetable stock
2 tablespoons cornstarch mixed with 2 tablespoons water
Salt & pepper to taste
Nevis hot sauce to taste
1 sprig cilantro
1/4 cup fresh grated coconut, toasted

Heat oil in a soup pot. Add chicken and curry powder and sauté for a couple of minutes. Add onion, carrot, celery, potato, ginger, garlic, and lemon grass. Continue sautéing until curry powder sticks to the bottom of the pot. Then, add coconut milk and bring to a boil while scraping the bottom of the pot. Add stock, return to a boil, and simmer until potatoes are soft.

When ready to serve, heat to a boil, add cornstarch mixture and cook. Season to taste. Garnish each soup bowl with a couple of leaves of cilantro and toasted coconut.

♧ Oualie Beach Hotel
Nevis, West Indies

Chef Patrick Fobert has been cooking in the West Indies since 1991. He is presently chef at Oualie Beach Hotel, a 22-room hotel in a quaint location on the beach. The hotel's 50-seat restaurant serves continental cuisine with a Caribbean flair. According the Chef Fobert, it's an ideal place to stop for dining and relaxation following a day of snorkeling, scuba diving, windsurfing, and deep sea fishing.

Chicken Soups

☐ *Green Papaya & Kalamugay Soup*

Executive Chef Bryan Ashlock puts a tropical twist on a classic chicken soup served in a Hawaiian paradise.

Makes 4 servings.

1 whole tomato
1-inch knob fresh ginger
2 fresh garlic pods
10 ounces, bone in, half split
  stewing chicken
2 green papayas, peeled &
  diced

10 whole black peppercorns
4 cups chicken stock
1 teaspoon patis
1 cup cleaned Filipino spinach

Chop fresh tomato into dime-sized pieces. Peel fresh ginger. Smash garlic to extract juices. Chop chicken into bite-sized pieces. Combine these ingredients in soup pot and sauté for approximately 5 minutes, until chicken browns. Keep covered. Add papayas, whole peppercorns, and chicken stock. Simmer for 1/2 an hour. Season with patis. Just before serving, place spinach on top of soup and push down. Do not stir dish, or it will become bitter. Serve immediately.

⌂ Sheraton Moana Surfrider
Honolulu, Hawaii

The Sheraton Moana Surfrider is listed as a distinguished Historic Hotel of America by the National Trust for Historic Preservation. Affectionately known as the "First Lady of Waikiki," the property opened on March 11, 1901.

The hotel features 790 rooms including 565 with ocean views, three restaurants including the classic Ship's Tavern with ocean-front views, two cocktail lounges, daily entertainment, an outdoor veranda, a casual oceanfront beach bar, and convenient poolside snack bar. Special amenities include a traditional afternoon tea, a seasonal beach barbecue, Shiatsu massage, and a traditional fresh flower lei greeting.

☐ *Warren's Chicken Soup*

Sandy Creek Manor House innkeeper, Shirley Hollink, loves good soups. She makes this home cooked, good-for-what-ails-you chicken noodle soup. Guests are enticed to the Manor with special packages like the Sweetheart Dinner Package, a Murder Mystery Party, and romantic Sleigh Rides/Carriage Rides pulled by Clydesdales.

Makes approximately 12 servings.

3 to 4 pound chicken
3 to 4 bay leaves
1 teaspoon bouquet garni
1/2 teaspoon coarse black
 pepper
1 large onion, chopped
2 stalks celery, chopped

2 large carrots, chopped
5 chicken bouillon cubes
1/4 cup fresh chopped parsley
1 pound sliced mushrooms
1 pound large egg noodles
1 beaten egg

Place chicken in a large soup pot and cover with water. Add bay leaves, bouquet garni, and black pepper. Cover and simmer for 1-1/2 to 2 hours. Take out chicken, remove meat and skin from bones, and cut into large chunks.

Add onion, celery, carrots, and bouillon cubes to the broth. Simmer until carrots are tender. Return chicken to soup pot along with parsley and mushrooms. Stir egg noodles into soup and swirl in beaten egg. Cook until tender. Enjoy with warm garlic bread and a glass of white wine.

⬜ *Ajiaco*

Caribbean Travel and Life *reports, "...return guests and people in the know always request the meal plan when staying at Ottley's."* Chef Pamela Yahn's *delightful meals, concocted at The Royal Palm Restaurant, are an eclectic combination of French, Spanish, Indonesian, Vietnamese, Mexican, and Chinese cuisines.*

Serves 8 generously.

5 whole chicken legs or 1 small whole chicken
16 cups water
3 tablespoons butter
1 stalk celery, minced
1 large onion, minced
2 bay leaves
1 tablespoon fresh parsley, minced
1/2 teaspoon freshly ground black pepper
4 potatoes, peeled & cut into 1/2-inch dice
4 ears fresh corn, cooked & kernels removed from cob
3 tablespoons cumin, if desired
Chicken bouillon to taste

Boil chicken in water until well cooked. Remove from stock. Reserve stock. Skin, bone, and break chicken into bite-sized pieces and reserve. Melt butter in a soup pot. Sauté celery and onions until wilted but not browned. Add reserved stock, bay leaves, parsley, black pepper, and potatoes. Simmer over medium heat until potatoes are cooked. Add chicken, corn, and cumin, if desired. Return to a boil. Adjust seasonings. If stock is not strong enough, add chicken bouillon to taste.

⌬ Ottley's Plantation Inn
St. Kitts, West Indies

Ottley's has been described as "upscale and low key." The inn sets on 35 acres of lush grounds that provide amazing views of the ocean, mountains, and gardens. *Rum & Reggae: the Insider's Guide to the Caribbean* named the inn "Best Hotel in the Caribbean."

Once an island sugar estate in the mid 1600s, the property still contains the ruins of the mill where sugar cane was ground before being boiled to make raw sugar. The pool and restaurant are located in the remains of the boiling house. The current two-story Great House sits on the foundation of the estate's original house and the English Cottage once served as a storage house for cotton which was also grown on the estate.

▢ *Tomato, Bean & Turkey Soup*

Chef Russell Stannard makes his turkey soup unique with the addition of tomato sauce, white beans, ham, and Parmesan cheese. This is a great way to make a heartwarming, not-the-same-old-turkey soup from any leftover bird after the holidays.

Makes approximately 10 to 12 servings.

2 cups diced onion	1 tablespoon salt
1 cup diced green pepper	1 teaspoon black pepper
1 cup diced celery	2 pounds cooked, diced
1 tablespoon ground garlic	turkey meat
4 tablespoons butter	1 pound diced ham
8 cups chicken stock	1 cup Parmesan cheese
8 cups tomato sauce	1 tablespoon dried basil
1 pound white beans, soaked	
in water overnight, then	
cooked until tender	

In a large soup pot, sauté onions, peppers, celery, and garlic in butter for 10 minutes. Add chicken stock and bring to a boil. Add tomato sauce, white beans, salt, and pepper. Bring to a boil and simmer for 30 minutes. Add diced turkey, ham, Parmesan cheese, and dried basil. Mix to incorporate. Adjust seasonings. Serve hot.

❧ Rabbit Hill Inn
Lower Waterford, Vermont

There's no wanting for comfortable accommodations and exceptional dining at Rabbit Hill Inn, a three-time winner of Uncle Ben's Ten Best Country Inns of the Year award. Established in 1795, the 21-room inn and restaurant are filled with love and attention to details. Many of the rooms feature fireplaces, canopy beds, and whirlpool tubs for two.

Innkeepers John and Maureen Magee describe Rabbit Hill's setting as "a time-forgotten rural village amid mountains." They take pride that all the food served is made "from scratch," except for the fresh pasta and the Ben & Jerry's ice cream offered nightly in addition to their homemade ice cream.

Turkey Soups

Seafood
Soups

☐ *Chef Al's Famous Chowder*

How do you know who makes a fabulous clam chowder? Just ask Regis and Cathy Lee and they'll tell you it's Chef Al Hynes. After sampling Chef Al's chowder, the pair invited him on their morning talk show and the rest is history. Chef Al credits his success to Cape Cod seafood, "This area has the best seafood in the world: lobsters, clams, scallops, cod, that's what people come here for." Here's his world-famous recipe.

Serves 8 to 10.

1/4 pound unsalted butter
1 cup chopped Spanish onion
1 cup chopped celery
6 ounces flour
3 (6-1/2-ounce) cans chopped
   clams
32 ounces bottled clam juice

2-1/2 ounces salt pork, scored
1 teaspoon clam base or 2 clam
   bouillon cubes
2 cups diced potatoes, cooked
2 cups half-and-half, heated
Salt & pepper to taste

Melt unsalted butter in a soup pot. Sauté onions and celery until transparent. Add flour to mixture. Cook for 5 minutes. Drain juice from chopped clams and mix with bottled clam juice. Heat juices and add to soup pot. Whip until smooth.

Add salt pork, clam base (or bouillon cubes) and clams to soup. Cook for 20 minutes. Then, add cooked potatoes to soup and allow to stand for 20 minutes. Remove salt pork and discard. Stir in heated half-and-half. Season with salt and pepper to taste.

⌒ Chatham Bars Inn
Chatham, Massachusetts

Chatham Bars Inn is one of the last of America's grand ocean-front resorts and a renowned Cape Cod landmark. The turn-of-the-century main inn sits gracefully atop a rise overlooking Pleasant Bay and the open Atlantic. Charming cape-style cottages dot the surrounding landscape.

A member of the Historic Hotels of America, Chatham Bars Inn features 3 distinctive restaurants. The Main Dining Room serves signature New England cuisine in classic elegance, with panoramic ocean views. The North Beach Tavern & Grille delights families and friends with its traditional favorites and cozy atmosphere. The Beach House Grill, on the water's edge, is ideal for summertime luncheons, clambakes, and festive beach parties.

☐ *Crackers Clam Chowder*

There are probably as many ways to prepare New England-style clam chowder as there are people who love to eat it. Crackers Seafood Restaurant's Chef Freddy Sepulveda's method combines plenty of flavor without the usual calorie-laden cream.

Makes 4 servings.

6 ounces smoked bacon
1 medium onion, diced
3 stalks celery, diced
4 ounces butter
1/2 cup flour
1 pound clam strips

3 cups clam juice
1 teaspoon fresh thyme
2 medium potatoes, diced
Salt to taste
2 teaspoons black pepper

Chop bacon and cook in a soup pot until done. Add onions, celery, and butter. Sauté. Stir in flour and cook for 5 minutes. Add clams, clam juice, and thyme. Cook for 10 minutes. Add potatoes, salt to taste, and black pepper. Continue cooking until potatoes are tender.

⌂ Crackers Seafood Restaurant
Orlando, Florida

In the late 1800s, central Florida was a wild and woolly territory filled with cowboys. They were soon nicknamed "Cracker Cowboys" because of the loud cracking sound made by their 20-foot long whips. Today, all native Floridians are called Crackers and Crackers Seafood Restaurant honors them by serving some of Florida's best fresh seafood and sensational pasta. Crackers is part of Church Street Station, Orlando's nighttime dining, shopping, and entertainment complex in the city's historic downtown.

⊓ White Corn Chowder with Curried Manila Clams

Loews chefs individualize a classic chowder recipe with spicy chili peppers and a subtle flavoring of curry powder.

Makes 6 servings.

2 ears white corn, kernels removed
1 cup minced white onions
1 tablespoon minced garlic
2 tablespoons olive oil
1 tablespoon butter
2 Anaheim peppers, roasted & seeded
2 tablespoons fresh chopped thyme

1-1/2 teaspoons curry powder
3 cups chicken stock
1 cup heavy cream
18 fresh Manila clams, rinsed
Salt & pepper to taste
Chopped chives for garnish
Diced ginger for garnish

Sauté corn, onions, and garlic in olive oil and butter in a soup pot. Add Anaheim peppers, chopped thyme, and curry powder to mixture. Cook until vegetables are soft. In a separate pot, place chicken stock, cream, and clams. Bring to a boil and cook until clams are fully open. Strain liquid from clams into soup pot of vegetables. Pull clams from their shells and set aside.

Simmer soup pot of vegetables, stock, and cream for 15 minutes. Purée and strain through a fine sifter. Add clams. Season to taste with salt and pepper. Garnish each serving bowl with chives and diced ginger.

⟳ Loews Santa Monica Beach Hotel
Santa Monica, California

Located on the edge of the Pacific Ocean, Loews is an oceanside city resort, with the blue sea one side and the colorful cityscape of Santa Monica on the other. The highly-rated television series "Baywatch" is filmed just a few steps from the hotel.

Set in an elegant and picturesque five-story glass atrium, Riva, the hotel's signature restaurant, specializes in sunsets and seafood served in a contemporary Mediterranean style. The casual Coast Cafe provides regional cuisine with a Pacific Rim flair during all-day dining with an outdoor terrace and spectacular ocean views.

Clam Soups

☐ *Manhattan Clam Chowder*

While it's not too difficult to find a good recipe for creamy New England-style clam chowder, there aren't as many for the tomato-based Manhattan-style chowder. Here's one from the Radisson's Chef Rafael Gonzales.

Makes 15 servings.

1/4 stalk celery, diced
1 yellow onion, diced
1/2 red bell pepper, chopped
1/2 green bell pepper, chopped
36-ounce can chopped clams
36 ounces clam juice
10 ounces canned tomatoes, diced
10 ounces tomato sauce
8 cups chicken stock

1/2 teaspoon whole thyme
1/2 teaspoon oregano
1/4 teaspoon cayenne pepper
1/4 teaspoon white pepper
1/2 ounce chicken base
3/4 ounce fresh chopped garlic
2 potatoes, diced
Fresh chopped parsley for garnish

Sauté celery, onion, and bell peppers until soft. Add all other ingredients except for diced potatoes. Cook for 1/2 hour.

Add potatoes and cook for an additional 15 to 20 minutes, until potatoes are soft. Garnish each individual serving bowl with fresh chopped parsley.

⚘ Radisson Valley Center Hotel
Sherman Oaks, California

Just over the hill from Los Angeles, in the San Fernando Valley, is the recently renovated, 206-room Radisson Valley Center Hotel. For their guest's recreational enjoyment, there is a full health club on the Penthouse floor and a heated outdoor pool and spa.

Windows Bar & Grill is an ideal place for breakfast, lunch, and dinner. Serving delightful California cuisine, the restaurant features an elegant Sunday champagne brunch buffet.

🗍 *She Crab Soup*

Grove Park Inn's formal four-diamond restaurant, Horizons, features innovative classic cuisine in a setting that offers an experience that appeals to all the senses, from fresh flowers and white linen to picture-perfect dishes where the food is artfully arranged and soft melodies float from a grand piano.

Makes 6 servings.

Butter	1/4 teaspoon salt
1/4 cup diced celery	1 teaspoon lime juice
1/4 cup diced carrots	Juice from 1/2 lemon
1/3 cup tomato paste	2-1/2 cups fish stock
1/4 cup flour, sifted	1/2 ounce crab base
8 ounces snow crab meat	1/4 cup sherry
1/2 teaspoon minced garlic	1/4 cup heavy cream
3/4 tablespoon paprika	

Melt butter and sauté celery and carrots. Add tomato paste. Slowly whisk in flour. Cook for 10 minutes, stirring constantly. Add crab meat, garlic, paprika, and salt. Cook for 5 minutes. Add lime juice and lemon juice. Whisk in fish stock and crab base. Bring to a boil, then reduce heat and simmer for 2 hours. Finish with sherry and cream.

ᚙ TheGrove Park Inn Resort
Asheville, North Carolina

The Grove Park Inn Resort, one of the South's oldest and most famous grand resorts, built in 1913, overlooks the Asheville skyline and the Blue Ridge Mountains. The resort, listed on the National Register of Historic Places, is a favorite year-round destination with splendid views, old world charm, massive fireplaces, and a long tradition of exceptional service and hospitality.

Completely renovated and expanded, the resort contains 510 guest rooms and a wide range of amenities including a par-71 championship golf course, indoor and outdoor tennis courts and swimming pools, volleyball, a full-range Sports Center, and for parents as much as for the kids, supervised children's programs.

This ultimate mountain resort offers exclusive special packages such as The Great Gatsby, named after F. Scott Fitzgerald, a frequent visitor to the inn more than 60 years ago.

⎕ Whiskeyed Crab Soup

Brian Poor, the executive chef at Chandler's Crabhouse and Fresh Fish Market, is one of the premier seafood chefs in Seattle. He has had the honor of preparing a miniature "Crabfest" at the James Beard House in New York City. This soup was served at the seafood event.

Serves 6 to 8.

1 Dungeness crab in shell, 2 to 2-1/2 pounds	Dash of Tabasco
4 ounces butter plus 2 tablespoons butter	1 tablespoon Worcestershire
3/4 cup flour	1/4 teaspoon Old Bay Seasoning
4 cups crab stock	1/4 teaspoon white pepper
3 cups heavy cream	2 teaspoons whiskey
1/4 lemon	1 tablespoon dry sherry
	Salt to taste

Clean the crab and remove meat from the shell. Reserve the meat. Use the shell to make Chandler's Crab Stock (see chapter on Homemade Stocks).

Make a roux in a heavy saucepan. Melt 4 ounces of the butter over medium heat. When the foam subsides, add flour all at once. Stir constantly and reduce heat to low. Continue to cook, stirring constantly, until roux is a blond color, approximately 5 minutes. Add crab stock, cup-by-cup, whisking thoroughly after each addition. Bring to a boil, then reduce to a simmer for 20 minutes, skimming frequently. Add heavy cream, juice from the lemon, Tabasco, Worcestershire, Old Bay Seasoning, and white pepper. Bring back to a simmer for 10 minutes. Add whiskey, sherry, remaining 2 tablespoons of butter, and reserved crab meat. Cook for 1 minutes to heat through. Salt to taste.

⟲ Chandler's Crabhouse and Fresh Fish Market
Seattle, Washington

Chandler's Crabhouse and Fresh Fish Market is reminiscent of an East Coast fish house with expansive views of Lake Union. Diners delight in viewing the live lobster and crab tanks next to the full-display kitchen. The menu is a seafood lover's paradise featuring such delicacies as House-smoked Seafood Sampler, Chandler's Dungeness Crab Cakes, Coconut Prawns, Whiskeyed Crab Soup, and Stuffed Baked Prawns. The Fish Market displays a selection of fresh seafood for retail sale.

⬚ Dewey's Crab Chowder with Beer and Muenster Cheese

Dewey's, a popular San Francisco sports bar housed in The Westin St. Francis hotel, serves over 50 different beers from every corner of the world. Any dark beer will work well in this chowder, but the chefs at Dewey's use Anchor Steam.

Makes 6 to 8 servings.

1/4 cup butter
1 onion, diced
3 stalks celery, diced
1 baking potato, peeled & diced
2 tablespoons chopped garlic
1 tablespoon chopped thyme leaves
1 tablespoon chopped parsley
1-1/2 teaspoons red chili flakes

1/2 cup flour
4 cups chicken stock
1/2 pound Muenster cheese, cubed
12 ounces bottled, dark beer
1/2 pound Dungeness crab meat, without shells
1/2 cup whipping cream
Salt & pepper to taste
Worcestershire sauce to taste

Melt butter in a soup pot. Add onion, celery, potato, garlic, thyme, parsley, and red chili flakes. Sauté for 2 to 3 minutes over medium heat. Sprinkle flour into pot and carefully stir until flour is absorbed into butter. Add chicken stock and simmer for 10 minutes over low heat. Stir to incorporate ingredients. Add cheese and beer. Simmer until vegetables are tender and cheese is fully melted, about 10 minutes. Stir in crab meat and cream and return to a simmer until crab meat is cooked through, about 5 minutes. Then, season to taste with salt, pepper, and Worcestershire sauce.

↻ The Westin St. Francis
San Francisco, California

When The St. Francis opened its doors to the public in 1904, the citizens loved its innovations and opulence. The hotel's luster is as bright as ever as it continues a $50 million renovation. The historic hotel has welcomed many guests of international fame and prominence during its 100-year history. Shirley Temple, Bob Hope, Jerry Lewis, Earnest Hemingway, Truman Capote, General Douglas MacArthur, Mother Teresa, all the U.S. Presidents since Taft, and England's Queen Elizabeth II are among the countless world-famous guests to lodge at The Westin St. Francis.

Crab Soups

⊓ Sweet Potato Corn
Crab Chowder

Sweet Potato Corn Crab Chowder is one of the delectable dishes served at the annual Stone Crab, Seafood & Wine Festival. The event, hosted by The Colony Beach & Tennis Resort, pays homage to the Florida stone crab. Americans consume close to 2.4 million pounds of the rich, sweet-tasting crab claws each year.

Makes 4 to 6 portions.

2 cups seasoned chicken stock	2 cups heavy cream
1 cup baked, peeled, mashed sweet potatoes	Ground cinnamon to taste Salt to taste
1 cup corn kernels	4 ounces crab meat
1/2 cup maple syrup	

In a heavy-bottomed stockpot, add chicken stock, mashed sweet potatoes, corn, and maple syrup. Bring to a boil. Add heavy cream and simmer for 20 minutes or until thickened to desired consistency. Season to taste with cinnamon and salt. Garnish with crab meat just before serving.

♧ The Colony Beach & Tennis Resort
Longboat Key, Florida

If any one place reflects the essence of resort living and luxury, The Colony Beach & Tennis Resort has to be among the list of top candidates. Overlooking the Gulf of Mexico, spacious, elegant suites, complete with kitchenettes, are filled with fresh flowers and tropical plants.

Children look forward to a new and different program of fun each day at the complimentary Kidding Around child care program while adults renew and revive at the resort's no-charge Fitness Center and Health Spa. Outdoor enthusiasts soak up some sun while playing tennis on one of 21 courts, bicycling along 12 miles of bike paths, snorkeling, sailing, windsurfing, and relaxing beachside.

The Colony's annual Stone Crab, Seafood & Wine Festival is an exciting weekend of culinary demonstrations, wine tastings, and spectacular dinner events given by some of the nation's most renowned chefs and world-class vinters. Unlimited amounts of ready-to-eat claws are available to feast on, along with other mouth-watering Florida seafood treasures prepared by guest chefs.

☐ *Robin's Salmon Bisque*

Rather than strive for perfect authenticity in recreating the ethnic dishes he loves, Chef Robin transforms each individual dish into his own, employing his love of food and unique taste.

Makes approximately 12 servings.

1/2 cup butter	1 teaspoon salt
2 cups sliced leeks	1/2 teaspoon pepper
1/2 pound sliced mushrooms	4 cups salmon, bones removed
1 tablespoon crushed garlic	& cut into 1/2-inch cubes
46 ounces clam juice	4 cups cream
4 cups crushed tomatoes	1/2 cup flour
1/2 cup chopped parsley	Fresh dill sprigs for garnish
2 teaspoons dill weed	

Melt butter in a large pot. Add leeks, mushrooms, and garlic. Sauté for approximately 5 minutes. Add clam juice, tomatoes, parsley, dill, salt, and pepper. Heat broth to almost boiling and add salmon. Cook salmon for approximately 3 to 5 minutes. Stir in cream and whisk in flour. Reheat. To serve, garnish with fresh dill sprigs.

⌇ Robin's Restaurant
Cambria, California

According to owners, Chef Robin and his wife, Shanny Covey, "We serve food from the heart." When they opened Robin's Restaurant in 1985 their concept was simple: to create a place where all kinds of people could enjoy a simple, delicious meal in a warm and friendly atmosphere at a reasonable cost.

The restaurant is housed in a cozy home where you'll find Asian curries alongside grilled seafood, unique pastas, and black bean dishes. Dedicated to quality, all meals are prepared using the freshest, most wholesome ingredients available. The result is an ever-changing variety of home cooked meals using eclectic recipes from around the world.

Salmon Soups

☐ *Mussel Chowder*

Fresh mussels will stay alive for up to 24 hours if kept cool and covered with a damp cloth. Discard any with broken shells or that don't close when touched. Mussels should be cleaned just before cooking. First scrape off any barnacles and pull off the tough, brown hairlike "beard." Then, scrub mussels well with a stiff brush under cold running water.

Makes 6 to 8 servings.

1 whole shallot, chopped	1 potato, peeled & diced
1 teaspoon chopped garlic	1 carrot, peeled & diced
2 cups white wine	2 pieces celery, diced
2 cups Pernod (a licorice-flavored liqueur)	1-1/2 cups heavy cream
	1 tablespoon thyme
2 pounds mussels, cleaned & bearded	Salt & pepper to taste

Combine chopped shallot, garlic, white wine, and Pernod in a large pot. Add mussels and steam until mussels open, approximately 4 to 8 minutes. Drain liquid into soup pot. Allow mussels to cool, then pick meat from shell and set aside. Add diced potato, carrot, and celery to steaming broth in soup pot. Cook until tender. In a separate pot, bring heavy cream to a boil and cook until it is reduce by half. Then add cream, mussels, and thyme to soup. Season to taste with salt and pepper.

ᗡ The Bellevue Hotel
Philadelphia, Pennsylvania

The legendary 1904 Bellevue Hotel is a masterpiece of French Renaissance-style architecture. In addition to its luxurious guest rooms, the Grand Dame of Philadelphia's historic Broad Street boasts several distinctive restaurants and a gourmet food court.

The Founders Dining Room, one of the "Top 50 Restaurants in the United States" according to *Condé Nast Traveler* magazine, presents inventive American and Continental cuisine from dawn to dusk. The restaurant's wine cellar contains the largest selection of French wines in the city. The Philadelphia Library Lounge is reminiscent of an intimate English gentlemen's club with dark woods, and imposing fireplace, and a collection of eclectic books by or about Philadelphians. The sun-drenched Ethel Barrymore Room offers elegant afternoon teas and sophisticated weekend entertainment beneath a 30-foot diameter dome ceiling.

⬜ *Anise Saffron Mussel Soup*

Chef Didier Tsirony has mastered the art of gourmet cuisine in top-rated restaurants from Paris, France to Washington, D.C.

Serves 4.

1 pound medium-size Penn Cove mussels, cleaned
1 chopped onion
3 cloves garlic
1/4 cup Pernod (licorice-flavored liqueur)
2 cups white wine
1 bouquet garni: 1 clove, 1 bay leaf, parsley stems, 1 juniper berry, & fresh thyme
2 cups clam juice
Vegetable brunoise, diced very small: 1/4 cup *each* carrot, celery, onion, leek, fennel, red pepper, & zucchini
2 tablespoons chopped garlic
2 tablespoons olive oil
Seasoning mix: dash of cumin, pistils of saffron, & salt & pepper to taste
3 cups heavy cream, reduced
2 tablespoons chopped dill
2 tablespoons finely chopped tomato
4 sprigs fresh dill or fennel

In a pot, put mussels, onion, garlic, Pernod, white wine, and bouquet garni. Bring to a boil, add clam juice and continue cooking, covered, for 2 minutes. Strain the juice and reserve. Reserve mussels in shells in a little cooking liquid.

In a second pot, on low flame, sauté the vegetable brunoise and garlic in olive oil. Stir in seasonings mix. Then add reserved cooking liquid and bring to a boil for 5 minutes. Mix in reduced cream and simmer for 10 more minutes. Add chopped dill.

Ladle soup into individual bowls and place 4 mussels in the center of each bowl. Set diced tomato and dill or fennel on top.

⤳ The Pfister Hotel
Milwaukee, Wisconsin

The Pfister, one of America's oldest hotels, opened its doors in 1893. A forerunner in modern technology, it was among the first hotels in the country to run entirely on electricity, using its own generators. The hotel was one of the earliest to have individual thermostat controls in each sleeping room and was the first completely fireproof hotel.

Now in its second century of elegance, the meticulously restored, luxury hotel, located just a few blocks from beautiful Lake Michigan, is within walking distance to the city's many lakefront festivals, speciality shops, and exciting theatre district.

Mussel Soups

⎕ *Bisque of Fennel with Belon Oysters*

Chefs at Grove Park Inn Resort's four-star Horizons restaurant prepare hot and cold soups daily as part of their classic cuisine menu and lavish buffets. Many of the resort's guests ask for the soup recipes. This one's a particular favorite.

Makes 5 servings.

5 medium shallots
16 to 20 Belon oysters
   (substitute domestic selects
   if needed)
3 cups diced fennel, bulb &
   stems
1 teaspoon fennel seed
2 cups diced leeks

4 cups clear chicken stock
8 cups heavy whipping cream
Salt & pepper to taste
Anisette (a liqueur made with
   aniseed - licorice-like flavor)
For garnish: aniseed,
   decorative crouton, &
   chopped chives

Peel and cut shallots in half. Toast on a pie tin in a 350-degree oven for 20 to 30 minutes until well browned. Purée in a food processor and set aside for later use. Shuck oysters. Reserve liquor and set oysters aside in a pie tin for later use.

Add fennel, fennel seeds, and leeks to a large shallow pan. Add chicken stock and bring to a high boil. When stock is reduced by 2/3 add cream and bring to a full boil. Lower to medium heat and reduce by 1/3. Remove from heat and strain through a fine China cup or food mill. Return to heat and hold at a simmer. Stir in roasted shallot purée. Salt and pepper to taste.

To serve, pop oysters in a high oven until edges begin to curl, about 4 minutes. Spoon a little of the oyster liquor and a splash of anisette into each serving bowl. Then add 2 to 3 oysters to each bowl and pour bisque over all. Garnish with a sprinkling of aniseed, decorative crouton, and chopped chives.

⬜ *Mr. Ford's Shrimp, Crab & Corn Soup*

Chef Bruce Ford's Shrimp, Crab & Corn Soup is perhaps the most frequently requested item on The Grand Dining Room's menu. The Jekyll Island area has an established reputation for excellent fresh crab and shrimp, and when Chef Ford works his magic with these two local ingredients and a few herbs from the hotel's herb garden ..... you have a taste sensation you'll remember for a long time. Here's his soup recipe.

Makes 1/2 gallon.

3 strips raw bacon, diced	2 ounces peeled pimento, diced
1/2 medium onion, diced	2 ounces peeled green pepper, diced
2 cups fresh sweet corn	
4 ounces margarine	
1/4 cup flour	1 pound raw shrimp, diced
2 cups fish stock	1 pound lump crab meat
2 cups chicken stock	3 cups half-and-half
1/4 teaspoon oregano	1 dash Tabasco sauce

In a large soup pot, sauté bacon and onions until clear. Stir in corn and margarine. Cook until margarine is thoroughly melted and clear. Add flour and stir until well blended. Add fish stock, chicken stock, oregano, pimento, and green pepper. Bring to a boil. Whip out any roux lumps. Simmer for 1 to 1-1/2 hours.

Add shrimp, crab, half-and-half, and Tabasco sauce. Bring to a boil. Adjust seasoning. Simmer for 10 minutes and serve.

⌇ Jekyll Island Club Hotel
Jekyll Island, Georgia

In 1886 Jekyll Island Club was founded as a private winter hunting retreat for society's wealthy elite by J.P. Morgan, William Rockefeller, and 50 or so of their friends. Over the years the Island became a gathering place for the nation's "movers and shakers." It's here at the Club, in 1910, that a small group of financial leaders met in secrecy to formulate a proposal that was the forerunner of the Federal Reserve Banking System. The first transcontinental phone call, actually a four-way conference call, participated in by Theodore Vail, president of AT&T, Woodrow Wilson, Alexander Graham Bell, and Thomas Watson, was made from the island.

Today, Jekyll Island Club Hotel is a full-service resort where people from all walks of life can visit what began as the "richest, the most exclusive, the most inaccessible club in the world."

⬜ *Lobster & Corn Chowder*

"Nevis has tremendous fresh ingredients, and a strong, interesting tradition of Creole cuisine," says Chef Jeff DeBarbieri. "I try to blend these two assets to create memorable and appealing dishes."

Makes 6 to 8 servings.

4 tablespoons butter
1 teaspoon chopped garlic
Dice small (corn kernel-size):
  1 medium onion
  1 medium carrot
  1 rib celery
  1 leek (white part only)
  1/2 sweet red pepper
  1/2 bulb fennel
  1 large cap portabello mush-
    room, peeled, gills scraped
Kernels from 3 ears fresh corn
2 tablespoons fresh tarragon

1 bay leaf
2 cups dry white wine
6 cups fish fumet, shrimp or
  lobster stock
2 large lobster tails, cooked,
  cleaned, & diced small
3 cups heavy cream
To taste: salt, black pepper,
  cayenne, grated fresh
  nutmeg
Garnish: fresh chive or chopped green onion

Have all of the above ingredients prepared and ready to go. Melt butter in a large saucepan over medium heat. Add garlic and sauté for 15 seconds. Add diced vegetables, corn, chopped tarragon, and bay leaf. Sweat this mixture for 10 minutes over low heat (do not brown). Add wine and stock and bring to a boil. Skim off foam that rises to the surface. Simmer for 5 minutes. Add lobster meat and cream and return to a simmer. Skim any foam. Season to taste with salt, black pepper, cayenne, and nutmeg. Garnish with fresh chive or chopped green onion.

⌂ Mount Nevis Hotel & Beach Club
Nevis, West Indies

The Mount Nevis Hotel & Beach Club is well known for its elegant accommodations and breathtaking ocean views. Under the guidance of Chef Jeff DeBarbieri, it's fast becoming known for its innovative cuisine as well. The hotel's restaurant overlooks the freshwater swimming pool and provides a panoramic vista of the Caribbean Sea. Thanks to Chef DeBarbieri's delightful blend of Continental and Caribbean dishes, Fodders hails the menu as "one of the island's most creative." The Beach Club restaurant features lighter fare and speciality pizzas in a casual tropical setting.

⬜ *Spicy Conch Bisque*

The Four Seasons Resort Nevis is a first class vacation destination in the West Indies. Their restaurants offer a variety of sumptuous dining experiences. A conch is a type of shellfish with a large coiled shell that is sometimes used for listening to the sound of "ocean waves."

Makes about 2-1/2 gallons.

16 conch, pounded & diced
10 liters fish stock
3 *each* red, green, & yellow
**   bell peppers, diced**
3 zucchini, skin portion, diced
2 red onions, diced
2 carrots, diced
Olive oil

8 ounces dry cognac
2 tablespoons thyme, chopped
2 jalapeño peppers, diced
1 teaspoon cinnamon
2 cups cream
Salt & pepper to taste
White roux for thickening

In a soup pot, cook conch in fish stock until tender. Sauté peppers, zucchini, onions, and carrots in olive oil. Deglaze with cognac and add to the conch soup. Simmer for 20 minutes. Finish soup with thyme, jalapeño peppers, cinnamon, and cream. Season to taste with salt and pepper. Thicken with a little white roux. If needed, more spices can be added to taste.

Chilies
&
Gumbos

☐ *Green Chili*

Union Station Hotel adds another pepper to its cap by being named Chili Maker of the Year. The best chili in Music City USA was created by hotel executive chef, Wilfried Comien. The culinary veteran credits the spicy honor to a unique pairing of savory ingredients.

Serves 6 to 8.

3 pound pork shoulder
36 ounces green chilies,
    canned or frozen
1 large roasted red pepper,
    diced
1 large green bell pepper,
    diced
2 large onions, diced
2 teaspoons garlic, chopped
3/4 cup jalapeños, chopped

1/2 cup plus 2 tablespoons oil
12 ounces beer
4 cups chicken stock
1 cup flour
1/2 teaspoon basil
1/4 teaspoon oregano
1/2 teaspoon cayenne pepper
Salt & pepper to taste
Grated Cheddar cheese for
    garnish

Slow roast pork shoulder until very tender. Allow to cool. Pull meat from bones in strips. Set aside.

Sauté vegetables in 2 tablespoons of the oil until translucent. Add pork strips. Deglaze with beer and cook to reduce. Pour in chicken stock and simmer for 2 to 3 hours. Make a walnut-colored roux with flour, remaining 1/2 cup oil, and spices. Mix into chili. Simmer for an additional hour or more. Salt and pepper to taste. Garnish with grated Cheddar cheese.

⌂ Union Station Hotel
Nashville, Tennessee

The turn-of-the-century Union Station Hotel has become one of the area's most popular accommodations. Visitors to the upscale 124-room Romanesque-Revival limestone building find themselves in another era. Built in 1900, the original Union Station served as the city's passenger train facility until 1976. It lay empty and dormant before reopening as a historical hotel in 1986. Today, it is listed on the National Register of Historic Places and offers top-quality service, decorative guest rooms, and rich and varied fine dining.

Chilies

⨅ *Christopher's Favorite Chili*

According to folks at Christopher Ranch, putting 30 cloves of garlic in one dish sounds like a lot even for a garlic lover, but the longer you cook garlic, the milder its flavor. When sautéing garlic, be careful not to burn it. If you do, it will have a bitter taste and you'll have to discard it and begin again.

Serves at least 15 people.

2 pounds "chili grind" hamburger
30 cloves Christopher Ranch Whole Peeled Garlic
80-ounce can chili with beans
15-ounce can "hot" chili with beans
16-ounce jar Christopher Ranch Garlic Salsa
1 bottle beer (optional)
4-ounce can diced jalapeños
6 hard tomatoes, chopped
1 yellow onion, chopped
1 green bell pepper, chopped
45 ounces canned kidney beans, drained
12-ounce can tomato sauce

Brown meat with 1/2 the garlic cloves in a large cooking pot. Add the rest of the ingredients and cook for 2 hours.

Refrigerate overnight. Cook for 1 hour before serving.

⟲ Christopher Ranch
Gilroy, California

There's so much garlic grown in Gilroy it's reported that humorist Will Rogers once exclaimed, "It's the only town in America where you can marinate a steak just by hanging it out on the clothesline."

Christopher Ranch is the nation's largest garlic grower, processor, and shipper. This Gilroy ranch distributes more than 25 million pounds of fresh garlic annually. Known as the "Stinking Rose," garlic plays a highly important aromatic and visible role in Gilroy's economy. Held each year in July, the Gilroy Garlic Festival is one of California's most popular events.

☐ *Award-Winning Buffalo Chili*

Everything Chef Moose Zadar of Silver Dollar City does is big. This stick-to-the-ribs, king-of-the-mountain kettle of chili served at Branson, Missouri's 1890s theme park, is no exception.

Serves a crowd.

6 pounds ground buffalo meat
1/4 cup sunflower oil
1/2 cup flour
3 cups water
1/4 cup minced garlic
3/4 cup chopped green bell
  pepper
3/4 cup chopped red bell
  pepper
1/2 cup chopped green chili
  peppers
1/2 cup chopped jalapeño
  peppers

5 cups tomato sauce
1/2 cup beef broth
3 diced onions
Spice mix:
1/2 cup paprika
1/2 cup chili powder
6 tablespoons ground cumin
1 teaspoon cayenne pepper
1/2 teaspoon black pepper
1/2 teaspoon white pepper
4 teaspoons salt
2 tablespoons oregano
2 teaspoons dried chilies

Sauté buffalo meat, sunflower oil, and flour together until meat is cooked. Add remaining ingredients and simmer for 1 hour.

⌂ Silver Dollar City
Branson, Missouri

A visit to Silver Dollar City seems like taking a trip back in time. The theme park entertains with over 50 musical shows, 100 authentic craftspeople who take rough forms of raw materials and carve, shape, hammer, and weave them into beautiful works of art, 60 unique shops, and 10 thrilling rides. Built on top of Marvel Cave, Branson nestles in the heart of the rich and colorful Ozark mountains.

Silver Dollar City's 12 restaurants serve down-home cooking and feature fresh-baked breads, regional specialities such as Ozark succotash, and home-style desserts like mountain-size fruit turnovers. Each day chefs demonstrate 1890s-style cooking over open fires in huge black kettles and 5-foot skillets.

Chilies

☐ Jacks Vegie Chili

In keeping with the concept of good-for-you food that satisfies the palate as well as nutritional needs, Kevin Koss, chef of Jumpin' Jacks created this vegetable chili.

Serves a hungry dozen, or more.

1/4 cup olive oil
2 cups diced onions
1 cup diced celery
1 cup diced carrots
1 cup chopped mushrooms
1 cup diced bell pepper
1/4 cup minced garlic
1/4 cup chili powder
1 teaspoon cinnamon
1 teaspoon cumin
1/3 cup flour

1-1/2 gallons vegetable stock
8 ounces black beans, cooked
    & rinsed
8 ounces chick peas, cooked
    & rinsed
8 ounces corn, with juice
1/4 cup honey
Salt & pepper to taste
Low-fat sour cream
Chopped fresh cilantro

Place first 10 ingredients in a heavy-bottom stockpot. Sauté until nice and fragrant. Dust with flour. Add vegetable stock, black beans, chick peas, and corn. Bring to a simmer. Stir in honey and continue to simmer for at least 1 hour.

Season with salt and pepper to taste. Serve with sour cream and chopped fresh cilantro.

⟨⟩ Jumpin' Jacks -- Cafe on the Water
Kohler, Wisconsin

The American Club resort hotel, originally built in 1918 to serve as a first home in a new world for immigrant workers at Kohler Co., is a gastronomic delight. Several distinctive dining establishments include a European-style wine cellar/bar, charming stained glass dessert house, rustic log cabins, and cosmopolitan dining rooms guaranteed to tempt any traveler.

One of the eateries, Jumpin' Jacks, serves a creative, good-for-you menu for breakfast, lunch, and dinner. This "cafe on the water" overlooks the indoor pool at Sports Core, the award-wining spa, fitness, and racquet complex. During the summer months, a floating dining raft, Jacks Splash, is set on scenic Wood Lake. Outdoor patio seating is available on the shore of the picturesque lake.

Chilies

⬚ Vegetable Chili

Travelers from far and wide visit Sprouts Restaurant at The Spa at Camelback Inn. After trying it, they rave about the delicious, distinctive Vegetable Chili. Here the resort shares their secret recipe so you can make Chef Steve Haughie's signature dish in your own home.

Makes approximately 6 servings.

1/2 Spanish onion, 1/2-inch dice	1/4 teaspoon curry powder
1/2 red bell pepper, 1/2-inch dice	1/4 teaspoon dark chili seasoning
1/2 green bell pepper, 1/2-inch dice	1/4 teaspoon cilantro
1/2 tablespoon olive oil	Salt & white pepper to taste
1/2 jicama, 1/2-inch dice	1/2 cup diced tomatoes
1/2 zucchini, 1/2-inch dice	2 ounces pinto beans, cooked slightly firm
1/2 squash, 1/2-inch dice	2 ounces black beans, cooked slightly firm
1/4 teaspoon cumin	

Sauté onions and peppers on high with olive oil until they start to become translucent. Add jicama, reduce heat to medium, and cook for 3 minutes. Mix in zucchini and squash. Cook for 2 minutes. Then, combine spices with vegetables. Sauté for 1 minute and add tomatoes and beans. Simmer for 30 minutes.

⌗ Camelback Inn Resort, Golf Club & Spa
Scottsdale Arizona

Arizona's award-winning Camelback Inn incorporates Pueblo-style guest casitas, three heated swimming pools, eight tennis courts, a 36-hole championship golf course, a 9-hole pitch 'n putt course, the Spa, a health and wellness facility for pampering the body and the mind, and 6 enticing dining options.

Always a favorite, Sprouts restaurant at the Spa is designed on the premise that good nutrition can be both delicious and hearty. The heart-healthy spa cuisine menu is built around pastas, whole grains, fresh fruits, vegetables, fish, and poultry. Two of the other popular eateries are Chaparral, for fine Continental dining and the Oasis Lounge & Patio, for snacks and light fare. The Camelback Golf Club restaurant serves breakfast and lunch daily, and the Kokopelli Cafe offers pastry and speciality beverages.

☐ Scallop Chili

Chef Russell Stannard of Vermont's Rabbit Hill Inn combines the distinctive flavors of roasted peppers with sweet, grilled scallops in his hearty chili.

Makes 24 (4 ounce) servings.

2 *each* red, yellow, & green peppers, cut in half, seeds & core removed
4 pounds scallops
3 tablespoons olive oil
1 large onion, diced
1-1/2 tablespoons minced garlic
2 jalapeños, diced
6 ounces tomato paste
2-1/2 cups fish stock
4 cups whole peeled tomatoes, crushed in the palm of your hand

1 pound black beans soaked in water overnight, rinsed, & cooked in fresh water until tender
2 bay leaves
1 teaspoon salt
1 tablespoon cumin
2 teaspoons dried thyme
2 teaspoons dried basil
1/2 teaspoon cayenne pepper
2 teaspoons chili powder
1/2 teaspoon red pepper flakes

Grill the half peppers until very well charred. Dice when cool and set aside. Grill scallops over very hot fire until rare but slightly charred. Set aside.

Heat olive oil in a large sauté pan. When hot, add onions, garlic, and jalapeños. Sauté for 7 to 10 minutes. Then, add diced peppers and tomato paste, stirring to incorporate. Stir in fish stock, crushed tomatoes, black beans, and all seasonings. Bring to a boil and simmer for 30 minutes.

Add grilled scallops and stir to incorporate. Cook for 5 to 10 minutes, then remove from heat. It's important not to overcook scallops when grilling or cooking in the chili because overcooked scallops become rubbery and tough.

Gumbo at its Best

A fragrant bowl of gumbo is Louisiana's favorite Creole soup. Most are created with a rich stock, fresh vegetables, top-quality meat, poultry, and/or seafood, spicy seasonings, and a flavorful roux (ROO). This thick, chunky soup is usually served over rice. Gumbo is similar to other soups in many ways but is made unique with the addition of several traditional, key ingredients. Here are our tips on making your own glorious pot of gumbo.

A roux is an equal mixture of cooked flour and oil or butter that's added to soups as a flavoring and thickener. Traditionally, a roux is made by heating oil or butter in a skillet, over moderate heat, and adding flour while stirring constantly as the mixture develops a distinctive nutty flavor. The longer the roux is cooked the deeper the color and the more intense the flavor. Generally, a light brown roux is used with dark meats, a dark reddish-brown roux is used with light meats and seafood, and a charcoal-brown roux is best for gumbos. One warning: if the heat is too high and you get any black specks in the roux, it's burned. Throw it away and begin again.

Two traditional thickening agents found in gumbos are okra and filé (FEE lay). Okra is a long, fuzzy-green vegetable pod which is usually sliced and added to gumbo for flavor and thickening. Filé powder is made from ground sassafras leaves. It has a particular pungent flavor associated with gumbo. It thickens in the same slippery manor as okra. It's often sprinkled into individual bowls of gumbo at the table because it loses its thickening power with boiling and reheating and tends to become slightly bitter.

People think of gumbo as hot and spicy. The amount of heat in the dish, and the combination of herbs, is a matter of personal preference. The seasonings are meant to enhance the flavors of the ingredients without overpowering the food. You can buy a Cajun seasoning mix, make up a batch of the Cajun Seasoning Blend included with the Spicy Cajun Gumbo recipe, create your own mix, or just add a little of this and a pinch of that as you cook. A few dashes of a good quality liquid hot pepper sauce adds immense flavor to any recipe.

Gumbos

Spicy Cajun Gumbo

Spicy Cajun Gumbo is a complete one-pot meal. Soup's On! *co-author, Gail Hobbs, combines chicken with hot Louisiana sausage and shrimp in her crockpot version of this Creole soup.*

Makes 12 servings.

1 pound boneless, skinless chicken, cut into strips
3 cups chicken broth
2 cups diced canned tomatoes
2 tablespoons Worcestershire sauce
1 teaspoon Cajun Seasoning Blend (recipe follows)
1 medium onion, chopped
3 medium carrots, thinly sliced
1/2 *each* red & green bell peppers, chopped

1 cup sweet corn
2 teaspoons minced garlic
2 tablespoons olive oil
1 pound hot Louisiana sausage
2 tablespoons all-purpose flour
8 ounces raw shrimp, shelled & cleaned
Salt & pepper to taste
Hot cooked rice
Filé seasoning

Place chicken, 2 cups of the broth, tomatoes, Worcestershire sauce, and Cajun Seasoning Blend in a crockpot on high heat. In a medium skillet, sauté onion, carrots, bell peppers, corn, and garlic in olive oil for approximately 10 minutes until softened. Add to crockpot. In same skillet, brown sausage on all sides. Reduce heat, cover, and cook through. Slice sausages 1-inch thick and add to crockpot. Pour out all but 2 tablespoons of the sausage fat. Add flour and over medium-high heat, stir constantly to create a very dark roux. Slowly add remaining 1 cup broth and stir until smooth. Mix roux into crockpot, lower heat, cover, and cook for 6 to 8 hours.

About 15 minutes before serving, stir in shrimp. Season to taste with salt and pepper. Serve over hot rice and pass the filé.

Cajun Seasoning Blend

1/4 cup salt
1 tablespoon cayenne pepper
1 teaspoon black pepper
1 teaspoon paprika
1/2 teaspoon chili powder

1 teaspoon granulated garlic
1 teaspoon onion powder
1 teaspoon nutmeg
1 tablespoon dried parsley

Combine spices in a small glass jar or shaker. Mix well. Store at room temperature.

⬜ *River Road Shrimp and Okra Gumbo*

This recipe has been in the Lanegrasse family since the 1800s. Vern Lanegrasse, The Hollywood Chef, remembers having it often during the summer months when okra was fresh and tender. Today, you can enjoy it all year long with frozen okra.

Serves 12.

1 cup vegetable oil	12 cups water or chicken stock
1-1/2 cups flour	2 pounds (35 count) shrimp,
4 cups okra	peeled & deveined
1 cup chopped celery	2 cups chopped green onions
2 cups chopped onions	1/2 cup diced parsley
1 cup chopped bell pepper	Salt & cayenne pepper to taste
1/4 cup diced garlic	Cooked rice

In a 2-gallon stockpot, heat oil over medium heat. Once oil is hot, add flour. Using a wire whisk, stir constantly until a golden-brown roux is achieved. Do not allow roux to scorch. Should black specks appear, discard, and begin again. When roux is golden-brown, reduce heat to a simmer. Sauté okra for about 15 minutes.

Add chopped celery, onions, bell pepper, and garlic. Sauté for approximately 3 to 5 minutes or until vegetables are wilted. Add water or chicken stock, one ladle at a time, stirring constantly until all is incorporated. Return to a medium-high heat to bring to a slow boil and allow to simmer for 35 minutes.

Add shrimp, green onion, and parsley. Season to taste with salt and cayenne pepper. Cook for an additional 5 minutes. Serve over cooked rice.

⌓ The Hollywood Chef
Hollywood, California

Vern Langrasse is an internationally known chef of haute cuisine, raconteur, a television and radio host, and culinary writer. A native of New Orleans, Langrasse had successful careers as a musician and television executive before deciding to combine his two loves -- cooking and show business. For over 20 years he has been known as The Hollywood Chef, appearing on his own television cooking shows and as a regular guest on *AM Los Angeles* and *The Morning Show*.

☐ New Orleans-Style Gumbo

If you're in New Orleans, you have to eat gumbo. This version, created by Chef Robert Krol, served in the restaurants in The Pontchartrain Hotel, is a favorite of local clientele and visitors.

Makes approximately 8 servings.

3/4 cup flour	Pinch cayenne pepper
3/4 cup oil	1 teaspoon Tabasco sauce
2 green bell peppers, chopped	1 teaspoon Lea & Perrins
1 medium onion, chopped	Worcestershire sauce
1/2 stalk celery, chopped	1 pound small shrimp
2 teaspoons chopped garlic	2 dozen oysters
5 bay leaves	1/2 pound crab meat
8 cups fish or shrimp stock	Salt & pepper to taste
10-ounce can tomato filets	1/2 cup filé mixed with 1 cup
with juice	water
1-1/2 cups sliced okra, sautéed	White rice, cooked

Make a very dark roux by mixing flour and oil in a pan over medium heat. Stir every 1 to 2 minutes until mixture is dark brown. Set aside. In a soup pot, sauté bell peppers, onion, celery, garlic, and bay leaves until tender. Add fish stock, tomatoes with juice, sautéed okra, cayenne pepper, Tabasco, and Worcestershire sauce. Boil for 45 minutes.

Stir in roux until dissolved. Add shrimp and oysters. Return to a boil. Add crab meat and salt and pepper to taste. Turn heat off. Stir in filé mixed with water. Do not boil after filé is in gumbo. Serve gumbo over cooked white rice.

ᴄᕫ The Pontchartrain Hotel
New Orleans, Louisiana

Constructed in 1927, The Pontchartrain was New Orleans' first luxury apartment hotel. Offering the services of a fine hotel and New Orleans' prestigious St. Charles address, The Pontchartrain immediately became home for many of the city's social elite. The Great Depression brought about the hotel's transformation into a commercial establishment. The original 84 apartments were made into 104 guest rooms. Today, original furniture and antiques are found in many of the hotel's guest quarters.

International Favorites

⊔ *Stracciatella*

Chef Roberto Marino's Italian egg drop soup is a classic favorite in one of Avalon's elegant seaside restaurants.

Makes approximately 8 servings.

1 pound chicken thighs & legs	**1/2 pound spinach**
1 large carrot	**2 eggs**
8 cups water	**4 ounces Parmesan cheese**
Salt & pepper to taste	

Boil the chicken and carrot in water in a large soup pot for about 15 minutes. Add salt and pepper to taste. Reduce heat to low and cook for an additional 45 minutes.

Remove the chicken and carrot. Bring chicken broth to a boil again. Add spinach and eggs. Stir for 2 minutes. Turn off heat. Add Parmesan cheese and serve.

♧ Ristorante Villa Portofino
Avalon, Catalina Island, California

Nestled in an oceanfront corner of the town of Avalon is the delightful Ristorante Villa Portofino. With its decor of Mediterranean peaches and creams, harbor views, and courteous staff, guests are served a selection of Northern Italian cuisine to the strains of soft Italian melodies.

Some of the dining delights supervised by Chef Roberto Marino, from Naples, include Insalata Partenope, an Italian salad with slices of tomatoes, fresh mozzarella, grilled eggplant, a touch of olive oil, and fresh basil with red vinegar; Crab Cakes -- served with Arugula and Strawberry Vinaigrette; Pappardelle Al Telefono -- with tomato sauce, fresh mozzarella, and basil; and Faggiano Brasato -- roasted pheasant with polenta, rosemary, and pheasant sauce. Desserts are equally enticing, with Tiramisu and Panne Cotta made fresh by Pastry Chef Andrea Giordano.

Hotel Villa Portofino, adjacent to the restaurant, has 34 comfortable rooms with a European flavor for the island's overnight visitors. It's close to the beach, shopping, and the world-famous Avalon Casino Building.

⬜ Escarole Orzo and Garbanzo Soup Menotti

Andy Lo Russo writes, "You can always tell if the main course is going to be a hit if the soup is good." Here he shares one of his best loved soups.

Makes 8 servings.

8 cups homemade chicken
  stock
1/2 cup orzo pasta (or pulcini)
1 cup garbanzo beans (chick
  peas)

1 medium head (1 pound)
  escarole, washed
Fresh-grated Parmesan
  cheese
Black pepper

Place chicken stock in a large stockpot and bring to a boil. Add orzo pasta and reduce to a low boil. Cook for 5 minutes. Skim off foam. Add garbanzo beans and cook for 4 or 5 minutes. Stack clean escarole leaves and chop into small pieces. Stir into to soup and cook, simmering gently, uncovered, for about 10 minutes. Serve with freshly grated Parmesan cheese and black pepper.

♻ Sing & Cook Italian
Santa Barbara, California

Andy Lo Russo loves to sing and cook simultaneously! Combining these two loves, he has produced a delightful cookbook that's loaded with some of his favorite Italian recipes, words to Italian love songs, and an audio cassette, "so you can sing while you cook."

Sing & Cook Italian contains over 100 authentic recipes from three generations of Italian cooks including antipasti, zuppas, insalatas, pastas, and la dolce vita, the sweet ending. The joy of spending time with family and friends while indulging in good food is emphasized. Special tips on low-fat healthy cooking with fish, and vegetarian pasta dishes are included as are a selection of Italian kitchen buzz-words and suggested menus.

☐ *Pasta Fagioli*

Pasta Fagioli is a traditional Italian bean soup. Filomena suggests, "You can use a mixture of different beans to add an interesting twist to each pot." Try adding kidney or pinto beans for variety.

Makes 6 to 8 servings.

1-1/2 cups dried cannellini
  beans (or 3 cups canned)
15 ounces dried short, mixed
  pasta
2 cloves garlic, chopped
1 stalk celery, thinly sliced
1 small onion, diced

4 tablespoons olive oil
8-ounce can crushed Italian
  plum tomatoes
Dried basil to taste
Salt & pepper to taste
Grated Parmesan cheese

If using dried beans, soak, covered with water, for about 4 hours. Drain, rinse, and cook in fresh water for 1 hour. Cook pasta al dente. Heat olive oil in a large stockpot. Sauté garlic, onion, and celery until onion is translucent. Add tomatoes and basil to taste. Simmer for about 15 minutes.

Stir in cooked beans. If desired, purée some beans to thicken soup. Add pasta with a little water. Season with salt and pepper to taste. Serve hot with a sprinkling of grated Parmesan cheese.

⌘ Filomena's Italian Kitchen
Oxnard, California

Filomena D'Amore is a second generation Italian restaurateur. Her father, Patsy, came to New York directly from Naples, Italy in the 1920s and opened restaurants in Brooklyn and Boston before traveling west to introduce pizza to Hollywood.

When Patsy installed a pizza maker in the front window of his Casa D'Amore restaurant he attracted the attention of Frank Sinatra. In addition to Sinatra, his well-known Villa Capri restaurant was a meeting place for many Hollywood stars. Marilyn Monroe and Joe DiMaggio were regulars. James Dean is said to have eaten his last meal there before taking that fateful drive. Jackie Gleason, Jimmy Durante, Bogie and Bacall, Sammy Davis Jr., Robert Wagner, and Natalie Wood all spent many happy evenings at Patsy's restaurant.

Filomena is following in her famous parent's footsteps by serving delicious Italian dishes, many made from Patsy's original recipes, in her small restaurant in the Channel Islands Harbor.

International Favorites

⬜ *Sylvia's Minestrone Soup*

This recipe was handed down to Sylvia Posedel from her Neapolitan mother when Sylvia opened her Italian restaurant 38 years ago. The original recipe is still used by Sylvia's daughters, who purchased the restaurant and dinner theatre from their mother.

Makes 8 to 10 servings.

1 gallon of beef stock
2 tablespoons salt
1 teaspoon black pepper
1 teaspoon oregano
2 tablespoons chopped parsley
3 large carrots, sliced 1/4-inch thick
5 stalks celery, sliced 1/4-inch thick
1/2 head cabbage, sliced 1/4-inch thick

2 cups chopped onion
10-ounce package chopped spinach
16-ounce can diced or peeled tomatoes
6-ounce can tomato paste
16-ounce can kidney beans
16-ounce can garbanzo beans
1 cup salad macaroni, uncooked

Bring beef stock to a rolling boil. Add the salt, black pepper, oregano, parsley, carrots, celery, cabbage, onion, and spinach. When the carrots are cooked, about 1/2 hour, add diced tomatoes and tomato paste. Cook for 10 minutes. Add the kidney beans, garbanzo beans, and salad macaroni. Cook until macaroni is done. Turn off heat and let stand for an hour before serving. Delicious served with Parmesan cheese and garlic toast.

↺ Sylvia's Authentic Italian Restaurant and Class Act Dinner Theatre
Portland, Oregon

Soup is usually what people think of when they think of Sylvia's Italian Restaurant. Ask anyone what's good at Sylvia's and they'll reply, "Sylvia's has the best minestrone." Shortly after being named Oregon's Restaurateur of the Year, Sylvia Posedel realized a dream of having her own theatre. In typical fashion, she acquired an adjacent tavern, bulldozed it, and built a theatre. Today, Sylvia's legacy lives on as diners enjoy Italian specialities while taking in award-winning shows such as *Driving Miss Daisy*, *Nunsense*, or *Dial M For Murder*.

⬛ *Ranch Minestrone*

Homemade soups and breads are a staple on the lunch menu at the Black Cat Guest Ranch. Manager Amber Hayward is the creator of this flavorful soup.

Makes approximately 6 to 8 hearty servings.

6 cups good dark stock
2 cloves garlic, minced
2 onions, chopped
4 stalks celery with leaves, sliced
1 or 2 green peppers, chopped
1 cup shredded cabbage
1 cup frozen niblet corn
2 tomatoes, chopped
2 cups kidney or brown beans, preferably home cooked, canned, if necessary

Chopped cooked steak, roast beef, or hamburgers (left-over barbecued meat is especially flavorful)
1/2 teaspoon salt
1/2 teaspoon pepper
1 tablespoon Italian seasoning
1/2 teaspoon cumin
1/2 teaspoon paprika
2 cups pasta, cooked

Add stock to a large soup pot. The stock can be made from any meat. The addition of onion skins while cooking adds color and flavor. Stock must be cooked and cooled a day ahead so all fat can be skimmed off.

Add garlic, onions, celery, green peppers, cabbage, corn, and tomatoes to the stock. Bring to a boil, then simmer for about 1/2 an hour. Add beans, amount of cooked meat desired, and seasonings to soup pot. Cook for an additional 20 to 30 minutes. Stir in cooked pasta just before serving.

♻ Black Cat Guest Ranch
Alberta, Canada

Whether you prefer to relax in comfortable surroundings, participate in outdoor activities, or savor natural flavorful family-style meals, Black Cat Ranch hospitality will fill the bill. The year-round ranch retreat is surrounded by colorful meadows and the stately trees of the rocky mountains. Its modern woodland lodge contains 16 comfortable rooms in addition to a large living room, fireplace, and dining room. Ranch hosts, Mary and Jerry Bond and Amber and Perry Hayward, invite their guests to experience Alberta in all her majesty while staying at the ranch.

International Favorites

⬜ *Carabaccia*

At Lorenza de Medici's villa in Italy, Deedy Marble studied with the noted cooking teacher and author. This Italian soup recipe is the result of her experience.

Serves 12.

6 medium red onions
6 tablespoons extra-virgin
  olive oil
6 cups beef broth
6 cups chicken broth
1 cup almonds, peeled &
  pulverized in a blender

1 teaspoon cinnamon
1 teaspoon nutmeg
Salt & pepper to taste
1 tablespoon powdered
  amaretto cookies
Miniature amaretto cookies

Peel and slice the onions finely. Sauté onions in olive oil in a deep saucepan on low heat until translucent. Add beef broth, chicken broth, and almonds. Simmer for 1 hour.

Purée in a blender. Add cinnamon, nutmeg, and salt and pepper to taste. Bring to a boil. Pour the soup into a bowl and sprinkle with the amaretto crumbs. Place a miniature amaretto cookie on top of the crumbs and serve.

⌇ The Governor's Inn
Ludlow, Vermont

As distinctive as the inn itself, The Governor's Inn is especially noted for its gastronomic fare prepared fresh with style, flavor, and panache. *Washington Post* food editor, Phyllis Richmond, called it "mysteriously delicious ... a bit of simple magic ..." Guests experience six-course dinners with inventive entrées like Bluefin Flambé with Gin and Juniper Berries, Oysters Newburg Under Glass, and Veal with B&B and Blueberries.

Innkeepers, Deedy and Charlie Marble, are both active in the preparation of the inn's fine dining. Deedy, who is the dinner chef, was trained as an artist and considers her present career an extension of that training. Charlie, who specializes in breakfast and funny stories, creates delectable treats like Rum Raisin French Toast garnished with rum raisin ice cream and maple syrup. Both cooks are professionally trained chefs with diplomas from L'Ecole du Moulin Roger Verge in France.

⛛ *Wigwam's Tortilla Soup*

The Wigwam Resort's Chef Jon Hill shares his version of this hot, south-of-the-border speciality.

Makes 10 servings.

2 cups diced celery	1 gallon chicken stock
2 cups diced red onion	1/4 cup diced green chilies
2 cups diced carrot	1 tablespoon chipotle chili
1/2 cup butter	6 corn tortillas, cut into strips
1/2 cup corn meal	Salt & white pepper to taste

Sweat celery, onions, and carrots in butter. Add corn meal to make a roux. Cook for approximately 15 minutes, stirring often. Add chicken stock and bring to a boil. Stir in diced green chilies and chipotle chili. Add corn tortillas. Purée in small batches and return to cooking pot. Season to taste with salt and white pepper.

✿ Wigwam Resort
Phoenix, Arizona

Don't let the name fool you. There's hardly a wigwam in sight. The absolutely top-notch Wigwam Resort has been honored with the *Mobile Travel Guide* Five Star Award 20 times for its welcoming hospitality and lodging amenities.

The resort offers fabulous feasting at several restaurants. The Terrace Dining Room serves Continental cuisine, the Arizona Kitchen dishes up Southwestern fare, and the Pool Cabana offers casual poolside refreshment. You can even arrange for breakfast in bed or a private hibachi dinner on the patio of your luxurious casita. There's plenty of outdoor activity available at the Wigwam including golf, tennis, swimming, shuffleboard, and croquet.

☐ *Tortilla Soup*

Chef Joe Cochran's cooking career spans the nation. He has served as executive chef for some of the best restaurants in Washington, D.C., Dallas and San Antonio, Texas. He has cooking experience in Escondido, Santa Monica, and presently, Riverside, California's Mission Inn.

Makes 6 servings.

1-1/2 teaspoons butter
1-1/2 teaspoons olive oil
1 large yellow onion, diced
28-ounce can diced tomatoes
1 jalapeño or serrano chili, diced
6-ounce can mixed vegetable juice cocktail
2 tablespoons chicken stock
2 cups hot water
3/4 teaspoon ground cumin
3/4 teaspoon paprika
Pinch chili powder

1/2 teaspoon white pepper
1 or 2 cloves garlic, minced
1-1/2 tablespoons tomato paste
1 cup chopped cilantro
1 tablespoon cornstarch
1 tablespoon water
6 (6-inch) corn tortillas
Oil for deep-frying tortillas
1 cup diced avocado
2 cups diced grilled chicken breast
1 cup grated Cheddar cheese

Heat butter and olive oil in a heavy saucepan until butter melts. Add onion and cook until translucent. Add tomatoes and continue to cook until soft. Add jalapeño and mixed vegetable juice. Bring to a boil. Stir in chicken stock and water. Bring to a simmer. Add cumin, paprika, chili powder, white pepper, and minced garlic. Cook, stirring occasionally. Add tomato paste and 1/4 cup of the chopped cilantro. Continue to cook while stirring occasionally.

Mix cornstarch with 1 tablespoon of water, then stir into soup and simmer until liquid is shiny, about 10 minutes. Meanwhile, cut corn tortillas into 1 x 1/2-inch strips and deep-fry in hot oil. Remove and drain.

To serve, distribute 1/2 cup of the avocado, 1 cup of the chicken breast, 1/8 cup of the chopped cilantro and half the tortilla strips among 6 bowls. Pour in hot soup and top with remaining avocado, chicken, cilantro, and tortilla strips. Serve Cheddar cheese on the side.

⌂ Mission Inn
Riverside, California

A National Historic Landmark, the Mission Inn is one of California's most dramatic historic buildings. The inn began as a two-story adobe guest house in 1876. In 1902 the expansion began that now incorporates design features from throughout the southwestern United States and several Mediterranean countries, with particular influence from the California missions.

Among the ornate architecture of the inn, the simplicity of fine dining is alive and thriving. Visitors to the Mission Inn can take advantage of the hotel's two restaurants: Duane's Prime Steaks and the Mission Inn's Restaurant. The inn's Presidential Lounge offers a friendly ambiance for a late afternoon cocktail or an after dinner night cap.

The list of famous dignitaries and movie stars who have stayed at the Mission Inn is a long one. President Benjamin Harrison stopped by to accept a bouquet of flowers in 1891, Theodore Roosevelt replanted one of the parent navel orange trees in 1903, Richard Nixon married his wife, Pat, in 1940, and Ronald Reagan honeymooned with his wife, Nancy, at the inn. Bette Davis got married there -- twice.

Muhammad Ali, Jack Benny, Jacques Cousteau, Henry Ford, Judy Garland, Helen Keller, Priscilla Presley, Ginger Rogers, Raquel Welch, Amelia Earhart, W.C. Fields, Ted Kennedy, Steve McQueen, Anthony Quinn, Oliver Stone, Will Rogers, Dr. Jonas Salk, Elizabeth Taylor, and Booker T. Washington were among the famous faces seen at the inn.

Occupying an entire city block and taking over 30 years to complete, the Mission Inn is now filled with more than 5 million dollars worth of antiques.

☐ *Albondigas Soup*

Maxine's Mexican meatball soup is reminiscent of a hearty, yet simple, South American meal-in-a-bowl.

Makes about 12 servings.

5 cans beef bouillon
4 cups water
2 (7ounce) cans Ortega Green
  Chili Salsa
1 onion, chopped
28-ounce can tomatoes, cut up
1/2 teaspoon *each* basil &
  oregano
1 teaspoon salt
1/4 teaspoon pepper

1/2 cup rice
For meatballs:
1 pound ground beef
1/4 pound pork sausage
1/2 onion, chopped
1 egg, beaten
1/4 teaspoon each salt, basil, &
  garlic powder
1/4 cup milk
1/2 cup cornmeal

In a large stockpot, mix beef bouillon, water, salsa, onion, tomatoes, basil, oregano, salt, and pepper. Cover and simmer for 20 minutes.

Meanwhile, make meatballs. Combine ground beef, pork sausage, onion, egg, seasonings, milk, and cornmeal. Form into walnut-sized balls. Add meatballs and rice to broth. Simmer very slowly, covered, for 1 to 2 hours.

⚘ Chef Maxine Cathcart
Yucaipa Valley, California

Since 1990 Chef Maxine Cathcart has shared her popular recipes with the readers of *The Valley Messenger*. Over the years, Darrell and Pat Teeters, publishers of the newspaper, have had hundreds of requests to publish Maxine's recipes in a cookbook. *Cuisine by Maxine* is a compilation of her own special dishes and recipes contributed by her numerous faithful readers.

☐ *Callaloo Soup*

St. Maarten's ethnic diversity is featured in two cookbooks written by John DeMers, Caribbean Cooking *and* Caribbean Desserts. *Callaloo Soup (Caribbean greens) is a flavorful sample shared by DeMers.*

Makes 6 to 8 servings.

2 pounds fresh kale
1/2 pound callaloo or fresh
  spinach
12 okra pods
1/4 pound salt pork, cut into
  thin strips
1/2 pound fresh lean pork,
  cubed

2 onions, thinly sliced
Freshly ground black pepper
  to taste
1 hot pepper, seeds removed,
  sliced
1 tablespoon fresh thyme
6 cups chicken stock

Pull all stems from kale and callaloo or spinach. Discard stems and roughly chop the leaves. Wash leaves thoroughly. Roughly chop okra. Place pork salt in a large, heavy soup kettle and sauté over medium heat for 10 minutes, rendering fat. Discard all but 2 tablespoons of fat. Add pork and onions to pot. Sauté over medium heat until pork is brown and onions are translucent, about 5 minutes. Add kale, callaloo or spinach, okra, black pepper, and hot pepper. Add thyme and stock. Cover and simmer 2-1/2 hours. Remove salt pork before serving.

☁ St. Maarten
Caribbean Sea

A 37-square-mile island, 150 miles southeast of Puerto Rico, in the Caribbean Sea, is the smallest land mass to be shared by two governments. French St. Martin is a commune of Guadeloupe, an overseas territory of France. Dutch St. Maarten is part of the Netherlands Antilles and the Kingdom of the Netherlands.

The tropical island is a vacationer's paradise and boasts 4,000 guest rooms from large resorts to small, intimate cottages. St. Maarten's melting pot of 77 different nationalities serves up eclectic dishes to visitors and natives from more than 300 restaurants. The native foods reveal touches from the French who have shared the island for more than 350 years. Familiarity may breed many things, and in St. Maarten recipe-swapping is clearly one of them.

◻ *Caribbean Yam Bisque*

Caribbean Yam Bisque is a favorite at one of the Farmers Market's most popular restaurants, The Gumbo Pot. They are rumored to serve an average of 10 gallons of gumbo a day. Restaurateur Charles Myers also owns the Big Sky Cafe in San Luis Obispo, California.

Makes 6 servings.

2 jumbo jewel yams	4 cups milk
2 cups diced onions	1/2 tablespoon sugar
1 tablespoons minced garlic	1 tablespoon, or more, roasted
Olive oil	ground coriander
6 cups fish stock (low-salt	2 tablespoons lime juice
chicken stock or a rich	Salt & white pepper to taste
vegetable stock may be used)	

Clean, peel, and dice the yams. Simmer in enough salted water to cover until soft but not falling apart. Drain and set aside.

Sauté onions and garlic in olive oil until translucent. Add cooked yams, fish stock, milk, sugar, and roasted coriander. (To roast coriander, cook the seeds in a dry, heavy skillet until they "pop," shaking constantly. Grind in a spice mill or with a mortar and pestle.)

Stir soup well while simmering for 20 minutes. Keep the heat low as not to boil. Transfer to the work bowl of a food processor and purée. Add lime juice. Adjust seasoning to taste with salt, white pepper, and additional roasted coriander.

⌂ Farmers Market
Los Angeles, California

The original Farmers Market was launched in July 1934, when 18 farmers parked their trucks on the Gilmore Ranch and sold fresh produce to local residents. Today's Farmers Market spans slightly more than 30 acres of land where 110 separate stalls filled with restaurants, fresh produce and food items, art galleries, books, clothes, and speciality shops cater to approximately 7,500 visitors daily. In any one day, 23 different languages may be spoken by sellers and buyers in this multicultural gathering place. Daily sales of wares are brisk including 1,000 donuts, 1,000 cups of coffee, 1,750 hotcakes, 200 pounds of fresh peanut butter, and 3,000 shrimp.

International Favorites

☐ *Yellow Thai Curry Soup*

Turnberry's executive chef, Todd Weisz, is tenacious regarding the restaurant's fresh, indigenous cuisine. He believes in serving five-star meals made with five-star ingredients.

Makes 6 portions.

1 tablespoon peanut oil
1 cup shallots, diced
1 tablespoon ginger, minced
2 garlic cloves, minced
1/4 cup lemon grass, chopped
1/2 cup leeks, chopped
2 tablespoons yellow Thai
  curry paste
1 cup dry white wine
4 cups chicken broth (or shellfish broth)

3 to 4 limes, juiced
3 tablespoons soy sauce
1-1/2 cups coconut milk
1 cup cooked sushi rice
1/2 cup pearl vegetables: 1
  each: zucchini & carrot
1 tablespoon fresh cilantro,
  chopped
1 tablespoon fresh mint,
  chopped

Heat peanut oil over medium-high heat in a heavy bottom sauce pot. Add shallots, ginger, garlic, lemon grass, and leeks. Sauté until translucent. Add curry paste and sauté for 2 to 3 minutes. Stir in wine and cook to reduce by half. Add chicken broth, lime juice, and soy sauce. Bring to a boil, then simmer 4 to 5 minutes over low heat. Add coconut milk and simmer. Coconut milk tends to break when heated, so blend soup before serving.

Prepare pearl vegetables by using a miniature melon baller to scoop out small balls of zucchini and carrot. Blanch vegetables in boiling salted water. Press 3 tablespoons of cooked rice into a small timbale. To serve, pop rice out and place in the center of a warm soup bowl. Ladle 1 cup of soup into each bowl, sprinkle with fresh cilantro and mint. Garnish with pearl vegetables.

♋ Turnberry Isle Resort & Club
Aventura, Florida

Turnberry's signature restaurant, The Veranda, is widely acknowledged as one of the best in Miami. It owes this enviable reputation partly to its "Floribbean" cuisine, a fusion of South Florida's tropical flavors with a savory blend of Cuban, Caribbean, and Latin American influences. Situated on 300 tropical acres, this stunning Mediterranean resort contains 340 ultra-luxurious guest rooms, two challenging Robert Trent Jones golf courses, and 24 tennis courts. The property contains a private Beach Club and a 117-slip marina for deep sea fishing and charter yachts.

International Favorites

▯ *Thai Chicken Soup*

Mike Magyar, one of the most respected soup chefs in the Pacific Northwest, has been at Fullers for several years. The acclaimed restaurant is popular for its internationally influenced and regionally inspired dishes. Signature meals include Moroccan spiced quail with preserved lemons and oregano, herb-encrusted sea scallops with curried pesto broth, and roasted beet and greens salad with shallot vinaigrette tossed with field lettuces.

Makes 8 to 10 servings.

1 ounce peanut oil
1/2 onion, julienne
1 rib celery, cut stalk in half
   lengthwise & slice thin
1 carrot, julienne
1-1/2 leeks, cut in half lengthwise, washed & sliced
4-ounce shiitake mushroom,
   remove stem & slice
1-1/2 quarts chicken stock
For the sachet:
   2 lime leaves
   1/2 stalk lemon grass
   1-1/2 Thai peppers
   2 slices ginger
   2 slices galanga (a root
      closely related to ginger)
   3 stems cilantro

1 can coconut milk
1 tablespoon fish sauce
1/4 cup lime juice
1/2 bunch Asian greens -- bok
   choy, tatsoi, or similar,
   julienned
Salt & pepper to taste
Marinated Chicken (recipe
   follows)
1/4 cup cilantro, chopped

Heat peanut oil in a soup pot over medium heat. Add the onion, celery, carrot, leeks, and shiitake mushroom. Stir until the onions turn translucent, about 10 minutes. Add chicken stock and sachet. Simmer for 30 to 40 minutes. Finish the soup with coconut milk, fish sauce, lime juice, and Asian greens. Salt and pepper to taste. To serve, ladle soup into hot bowls. Place a heaping spoon of chicken in the center of the bowl. Garnish with chopped cilantro.

Marinated Chicken

4 lime leaves, crushed slightly	1 tablespoon cilantro, chopped
1 stalk lemon grass, sliced	1/4 cup white wine
2 Thai peppers, chopped	Juice of 1 lime
3 slices ginger	2 chicken breasts
3 slices galanga	1 tablespoon olive oil

In a bowl, combine all ingredients except chicken breasts and olive oil. Mix well. Place chicken breasts in mixture and marinate in the refrigerator for 2 hours.

Heat 1 tablespoon of olive oil in a sauté pan over medium heat. Add the chicken, skin side down, and cook for 8 minutes. Turn chicken and continue cooking for another 5 minutes. Remove chicken from the pan and cool. Cut chicken breasts into small dice.

 **Fullers**
Seattle, Washington

Fullers restaurant, in the Sheraton Seattle Hotel & Towers, is well-known for its upscale dining in a comfortable, nonsmoking environment. The restaurant was named after Dr. Richard E. Fuller, the founder of the Seattle Art Museum. The Sheraton has one of the largest permanent public/private collections of contemporary art in the Pacific Northwest. More than 2,000 original works of art, valued at over $1.5 million, are displayed at the hotel and in Fullers restaurant.

☐ *Russian Sauerkraut Soup*

From The Lowfat Jewish Vegetarian Cookbook *by Debra Wasserman, this vegetarian soup's broth is a combination of tomato purée, vegetable broth, and sauerkraut juice. Wasserman suggests adding caraway seeds for a flavor that's absolutely delicious. Root vegetables are eaten often in Russia.*

Serves 8.

15-ounce can tomato purée
8 cups vegetable broth
16-ounce can or jar sauerkraut
1 onion, peeled & finely chopped
2 turnips (about 1 pound), peeled & cubed

3 carrots, peeled & finely chopped
1 teaspoon caraway seeds
Salt & pepper to taste

Place all ingredients in a large covered pot and bring to a boil. Reduce heat and cook for 1 hour. Serve hot with fresh bread.

⌬ Debra Wasserman
Baltimore, Maryland

Author Debra Wasserman serves up deliciously healthy dishes in *The Lowfat Jewish Vegetarian Cookbook.* Featured are 150 lowfat international recipes including 33 suitable for Passover.

Wasserman's book contains recipes to feast upon without guilt. Included are Czechoslovakian Noodles with Poppy Seeds and Romanian Apricot Dumplings. Wasserman celebrates meatless meals with Eggless Challah and Mock Chopped Liver. She tells of savoring Potato Knishes, Indian Curry, and Greek pastry. Each recipe contains a nutritional analysis.

The cookbook includes Rosh Hashanah dinner suggestions, a glossary of foods used in Jewish vegetarian cooking, lists of top 10 recipes for calcium and iron, and a bibliography for those who want to learn more about healthy Jewish vegetarian cookery.

Debra Wasserman is the author of *No-Cholesterol Passover Recipes, Simply Vegan,* and *Vegetarian Journal's Guide to Natural Foods Restaurants in the United States.and Canada.*

▯ *Brazilian Black Bean Soup*

Most cooks prepare soup using electricity or gas. An earth-friendly alternative is to cook with a sunstove. The fuel is free, and the soup can simmer for a half day or more. Here's a recipe from Bill and Melody Rockett, owners of Blackhawk Solar Access store. The recipe's ideal for the sunstove because of the long, slow cooking time required. The Rocketts tell us, "Everyone should experiment with sunstove cooking. The more people try it, the more they like it."

Makes approximately 12 servings.

1-1/2 cups dried black beans	2 slices bacon, cubed
1 onion, minced	1/2 cup orange juice
1 clove garlic, finely minced	1/2 cup red wine
or crushed	Salt & chili pepper to taste
1-3/4 pounds lean pork or beef,	Cooked rice
cut in 2-inch cubes	Orange slices for garnish
3/4 pound chorizo (garlic	
seasoned sausage)	

Soak beans in water overnight. Drain and cover with fresh water. Add onion and garlic and cook in a covered pot for at least 2 hours. Place cubed meat, whole sausage, and cubed bacon with a small amount of water in a large pan. Bring to a boil and simmer for 5 minutes. Add meats to beans and simmer for another 2 hours.

Stir in orange juice and wine. Continue simmering for an additional 30 minutes. Remove chorizo sausage and slice in 1/2-inch rounds. Save some rounds for garnish and return the rest to soup. Season to taste with salt and chili pepper. Serve on a bed of rice. Garnish with slices of sausage and orange.

௹ Solar Cook-off
Taylorsville, California

As our world approaches the next millennium, many folks are taking a longer look at ways to conserve, recycle, and make better use of the earth's limited resources. The Solar Cook-Off is an annual celebration focusing on utilizing the sun's energy and preserving the environment.

Throughout the event, 30 to 50 solar chefs cook delightfully delicious meals using sunstoves. They share tasty dishes and recipes for soup, appetizers, casseroles, lasagna, and whole turkeys with each other and interested members of the public during the two-day celebration of the sun.

☐ *Moroccan Lamb and Lentil Soup*

Chef Mohammed Zaidan delights guests daily with creative menus influenced by the season. His creative dishes are characterized by unusual combinations of flavors and textures.

Makes approximately 8 servings.

2 tablespoons garlic
1 onion, chopped
1 pound lamb, trimmed and
  cut into cubes
1 tablespoon olive oil
1 carrot, diced
1 celery rib, diced
1 green pepper, diced
2 pounds tomatoes, peeled,
  seeded, & chopped

1 teaspoon turmeric
Pinch saffron
1 teaspoon cinnamon
1/4 teaspoon ground ginger
1 cup (about 6 ounces) lentils
8 cups water
Salt & pepper to taste
1/4 cup chopped cilantro
1/4 cup chopped parsley
Lemon wedges for garnish

Sauté garlic, onion, and lamb in olive oil for three minutes. Add vegetables, dry spices, and lentils. Stir to coat. Pour in water and simmer for up to 1-1/2 hours.

Season midway through cooking with salt and pepper, then add chopped cilantro and parsley. When ready to serve, garnish with lemon wedges.

♧ The Fearrington Market Cafe
Pittsboro, North Carolina

One of the South's most celebrated restaurants, The Market Cafe, sits in the midst of a country village. The historic heart of Fearrington is a 200-year-old family dairy farm, symbolized by the original barn and silo. Many former farm buildings have been adapted to new uses in the village center.

The Market Cafe, located in the old farm granary, provides diners with a casual, comfortable atmosphere. The cafe's philosophy stresses that guests should experience a simple, yet interesting, meal. Chef Zaidan's sample entrées include grilled free-range chicken with saffron; Israeli couscous risotto with shrimp; and braised lamb with Northern white beans. Pastry chef Kelly Contant pampers diners with delicious, ample servings of freshly-prepared cakes, cookies, brownies, and other delectable treats.

⊓ *Tahitian Crab Meat Soup*

Chef Sam Choy says, "This is my favorite soup. The coconut gives it a taste of the South Pacific, while the spinach and crab meat make it so elegant and delicious. I love to serve this soup on a cold night with warm bread."

Makes approximately 6 servings.

**2 cups diced onion
1/4 cup butter
2 tablespoons flour
2 cups heavy cream
1-1/2 cups chicken stock
2 cups coconut milk**

**2 cups frozen spinach, thawed
  or 3 cups chopped fresh
  spinach, washed & steamed
1-1/2 cups crab meat
Salt & white pepper to taste**

In a large saucepan, sauté onion in butter until translucent. Stir in flour and blend well. Add heavy cream and chicken stock. Simmer for 5 minutes, stirring frequently. Stir in coconut milk, spinach, and crab meat. Cook for 3 minutes, stirring frequently. Season to taste with salt and white pepper.

⌓ Sam Choy's Restaurants
Honolulu, Hawaii

"When someone asks me 'What is Hawaii Regional Cuisine?' I tell them it's where East meets West in Hawaii," says Chef Sam Choy. His love of cooking began as a youngster in elementary school when he helped his father cater Saturday luaus. He inherited much of his fondness for island food from his father, who ran Sam's Place, the family restaurant. Choy's Hawaiian-German mother whet his appetite for home-style dishes like creamed, baked chicken, and old-fashioned pot roasts.

Chef Choy now cooks in his own popular, world-famous restaurants. His cookbooks, *Sam Choy's Cuisine Hawaii* and *With Sam Choy*, offer recipes not only for island people, but also for all who enjoy good food.

☐ *Crowdie*

This proves it. You can make soup out of anything. Crowdie, an oatmeal soup, is a Scottish recipe from the cookbook Auld Favorites -- Recipes from the Members and Friends of the Scottish Society of the Pikes Peak Region. *The society members celebrate their Scottish heritage each year during the Pikes Peak Highland Games and Celtic Festival in Colorado Springs, Colorado.*

Makes 4 servings.

4 cups meat or chicken stock, well-skimmed of fat
1/2 cup fine oatmeal
Cold water

1 onion, finely chopped
Salt, pepper, & sugar to taste
Parsley or chives for garnish

Bring stock to a boil. If oatmeal is not finely ground, whirl in a blender or food processor for a few seconds, then mix with enough cold water to make a slightly runny paste. Pour slowly into the boiling stock, stirring all the while. Bring to a simmering point again. Add onion and seasonings to taste. Cook for about 30 minutes. Sprinkle with chopped parsley or chives before serving.

Chilled
Soups

🍞 *Gazpacho*

A cup of chilled Spanish vegetable soup is a welcome sight on a hot summer day. Although Chef Bernard Axel's list of ingredients appears long, about half are seasonings and the recipe is fairly quick to make.

Makes approximately 10 to 12 servings.

1 large can of V-8 juice
3 tablespoons olive oil
3 tablespoons fresh lime juice
1-1/2 tablespoons Worcestershire sauce
3 cucumbers, peeled, seeded,
  & chopped
1 green bell pepper, chopped
1 red bell pepper, chopped
1 yellow bell pepper, chopped
1 bunch scallions, top only,
  chopped
1-1/2 teaspoons seasoned salt,
  or more, to taste

1 teaspoon fresh-ground
  black pepper
1/2 teaspoon cayenne pepper
1/2 teaspoon sweet Hungarian
  paprika
1-1/2 tablespoons fresh
  chopped parsley
Powdered or granulated
  garlic to taste
4 tablespoons dry vermouth or
  vodka, or more to taste
Sour cream for garnish
Caviar for garnish

Combine all ingredients in a large container. Chill for 4 hours, or more. If desired, garnish individual serving bowls with sour cream and a sprinkling of caviar.

🍴 Christian's Restaurant
Birmingham, Alabama

Award-winning Christian's Restaurant delights local diners and Tutwiler Hotel guests with tastes of Europe, the Southeast, and Alabama. According to executive chef and owner, Bernard Axel, "We're the only place in town where diners can celebrate Birmingham's rich history, enjoy regional specialities, and experience culinary delicacies from the Old World." Ladies are charmed with "good old Southern hospitality" when, during the dinner hour, they're are offered a one-of-a-kind red corduroy cushion for their feet.

Chef Axel notes the restaurant changes its lunch and dinner menu daily, so guests can take advantage of seasonal foods. Fresh seafood is brought in each day and certified black Angus beef is one of the restaurant's claims to fame.

Gazpachos

☐ Gold Gazpacho

A bright spring day is the perfect time for a cup of chilled Gold Gazpacho. Chef Steve Haughie of Sprouts restaurant at the Spa at Camelback Inn, brings this popular recipe from his kitchen to yours.

Makes 2 servings.

2 yellow tomatoes
2 peeled cucumbers
1 green pepper, seeded
1/2 peeled white onion
1/2 clove garlic
1-1/2 ounces olive oil
1-1/2 ounces red wine vinegar
1/2 cup V-8 juice

Dash of Tabasco sauce
Salt & pepper to taste
For garnish: diced tomatoes,
  diced jicama, diced red
  pepper, diced red onion &
  chopped chives

Place all ingredients in a blender. Blend until smooth. Chill. Garnish with tomatoes, jicama, red pepper, red onions, and chopped chives.

Gazpachos

☐ *Creamy Gazpacho*

Chef Anton Brunbauer's chilled Creamy Gazpacho offers a cool respite from the sizzling Arizona sun.

Serves 6 to 8.

5 medium-sized fresh, ripe tomatoes, coarsely chopped
1 English cucumber, peeled & sliced
1 large red onion, coarsely chopped
1 large red pepper, seeded & coarsely chopped
1 tablespoon chopped garlic
4 cups cold water
2-1/2 cups crumbled dried French bread

1/4 cup olive oil
1/4 cup red wine vinegar
1 tablespoon tomato paste
Ground cumin to taste, between 1 & 2 teaspoons
Salt to taste
For garnish: 1 cup of 1/8-inch bread cubes, 1/2 cup finely diced cucumbers, & 1/2 cup finely diced green pepper
1/2 cup finely diced, seeded tomato

In a large bowl, mix all of the ingredients except for garnish. Ladle 3 to 4 cups at a time into a blender. Blend at high speed for 1 to 2 minutes. Strain the mixture through a sieve into a bowl. Chill well for 3 to 4 hours.

Before serving, whisk the soup lightly. To serve, ladle chilled soup into individual soup bowls. Sprinkle with garnish.

♧ Hyatt Regency Scottsdale
Scottsdale, Arizona

A variety of dining experiences, from a snack at an open-air cafe to a gourmand dinner, are provided the guests of the Hyatt Regency Scottsdale. The hotel's speciality restaurant, Golden Swan, has been named one of the "Outstanding Restaurants of the World" by *Travel-Holiday* magazine.

Each Sunday, a special buffet, served right in the kitchen, provides a fun interaction between guests and the chefs. Not only are guests able to enjoy the chefs creative talents but also to view the "masters" at work and taste culinary delights hot off the line.

For a touch of Venice in the Arizona desert, Ristorante Sandolo is a casual Italian bistro where the pasta dishes are served by singing employees in a fun and relaxed setting.

Gazpachos

⎰ *Pineapple Gazpacho*

Award-winning chefs, Gale Gand and Rick Tramonto, share a love for creating superb food at their two Chicago area restaurants, Trio and Brasserie T. One of the culinary world's most revered couples, they are among the nation's top chefs who attend the annual Stone Crab, Seafood & Wine Festival. The event is hosted by The Colony Beach & Tennis Resort located on the Gulf Coast of Florida. Chilled Pineapple Gazpacho is one of the duo's signature recipes served during the 6th annual festival.

Yields 4 servings.

1 cup peeled, seeded, & chopped cucumber
1/4 cup chopped red bell pepper
1/4 cup chopped yellow bell pepper
1 teaspoon minced jalapeño pepper

1/8 cup chopped Vidalia or Maui onion
1 cup peeled pineapple meat
1 tablespoon flat leaf parsley
1/2 cup pineapple juice
1 pinch salt
1/4 cup stone crab claw meat

Place cucumber, red bell pepper, yellow bell pepper, jalapeño pepper, onion, pineapple meat, and parsley in a blender. Add pineapple juice and salt. Blend until mixture is liquefied. Garnish with crab meat. Chill before serving.

☐ Cool 'N Spicy Green Tomato Soup with Crab & Country Ham

Warm-up and cool-off with Chef Ben Barker's spicy chilled soup.

Makes 12 servings.

5 ounces country ham
1/2 cup vegetable oil
2 medium onions, sliced thin
6 whole peeled cloves garlic
4 green Anaheim chilies
2 green pasilla chilies
2 jalapeños, stemmed, sliced
2 bay leaves
3-1/2 pounds firm, green tomatoes, cored, cut into eighths
6 cups shrimp stock or home-made chicken stock

1 handful fresh basil leaves
3 tablespoons lemon juice
1-1/2 tablespoons Tabasco
Salt to taste
1 pound crab meat, picked over
1-1/2 cups sour cream
1 cup fresh tomato concasse with 6 tablespoons capers, chopped
1/2 cup sliced scallions

Julienne ham and cook in vegetable oil until crisp and golden. Drain and set aside. Return oil to pot. Cook onion in oil over moderate heat until soft but not colored. Add garlic, chilies, and bay leaves. Cook for 5 minutes. Mix in tomatoes and stock. Bring to a boil then, reduce to a simmer until tomatoes soften. Remove bay leaves and add basil. Purée soup in batches in a blender.

Chill. Season with lemon juice, salt, and Tabasco sauce. To serve, place crab meat in chilled bowls. Ladle soup into bowls. Garnish with sour cream, diced ripe tomato and capers, reserved country ham, and sliced scallions.

⌂ Magnolia Grill
Durham, North Carolina

Ben Barker and his wife, Karen, are the owners of the five-star Magnolia Grill restaurant. According to *Food & Wine* magazine, Ben Barker is "one of the ten best chefs in America ... Barker is still stirring things up, putting a global spin on the flavorful memories of his Carolina childhood." Karen Barker is the restaurant's gifted pastry chef, and she delights diners with her dreamy desserts. Both of the chefs are graduates of the Culinary Institute of America.

☐ *Olde English Parsley Soup*

This 100-year-old recipe is a fine example of how pure and simple English cooking can be. Parsley Soup is from the family recipe files of Mavis Caffrey, an enthusiastic organic vegetable and herb gardener. She was born and raised in Coventry, England.

Makes 4 servings.

1 small onion, sliced	2 cups chicken broth
1 tablespoon butter	2 cups milk
1 medium potato, diced	Cream to taste
1 bunch fresh parsley, leafy part only, chopped	Salt & pepper to taste
	Fresh parsley for garnish

In a medium-sized soup pot, cook sliced onion in melted butter just until transparent. Add diced potato and chopped fresh parsley. Pour in chicken broth. Simmer for 1/2 hour.

Allow to cool slightly. Purée in a blender. Add milk, and cream to suit your taste. Season to taste with salt and pepper. To serve, garnish with fresh parsley.

☐ Cauliflower-Buttermilk Soup

Christophe Barbier, executive chef of Mark's Restaurant, provides consistently fine fare to sophisticated diners who want more than standard hotel food. New York Times food critic, Bryan Miller, wrote that Mark's offers "some sophisticated, contemporary cooking that is on par with the better independent restaurants in town."

Serves 8.

1 Spanish onion, thinly sliced
2 tablespoons sweet butter
2 heads cauliflower, roughly cut
2 Idaho potatoes, peeled & roughly cut
2 cups clam juice

4 cups buttermilk
Salt & white pepper to taste
1 small bunch dill, finely chopped
Buckwheat blini, 1 cup crème fraîche & black American caviar on the side

In a large pot, sweat onion in butter until translucent. Add cauliflower and potatoes. Cook for 2 minutes. Pour in clam juice, then buttermilk. Simmer for 20 minutes until cauliflower is cooked.

Blend, then strain the soup. Season with salt and pepper. Sprinkle with some finely chopped dill. Serve on the side with a buckwheat blini, a dollop of crème fraîche, and a teaspoon of black American caviar. May be served hot or cold.

♻ The Mark
New York, New York

One of Manhattan's elite cadre of fine hotels, The Mark is located in the heart of New York's most fashionable neighborhood, the Upper East Side historic district. The hotel is conveniently accessible to Central Park, the Metropolitan Museum of Art, the Guggenheim, and Whitney and Frick museums. Within walking distance are the distinctive fashion boutiques of Givenchy, Ralph Lauren, Armani, and Gianni Versace.

The Mark's accommodations include 120 guest rooms and 60 suites, some with 2 bedrooms. Among the hotel's numerous amenities are twice-daily maid service, nightly turndown, concierge assistance, and in-room business services. A "wellness suite" offers guests the use of state-of-the-art exercise equipment and sauna and steam room facilities.

☐ *Roasted Poblano Vichyssoise*

Chef John Bobrick has traveled a long way from the New York deli on the east coast where his love of cooking began. He graduated from the Culinary Institute of America, and followed his heart to the Southwest. He provides Santa Fe with some fine upscale regional cuisine.

Makes 8 servings.

1 tablespoon olive oil	1/2 bunch thyme
1 yellow onion, sliced	Salt, pepper, & cayenne
3 whole jalapeño peppers	pepper to taste
7 poblano peppers, seeded	4 cups cream
2 cloves garlic	For garnish: herbed croutons,
10 Idaho potatoes	crème fraîche, or marinated
8 cups chicken stock	vegetables
1 bunch parsley, chopped	

In a large stockpot, heat oil until smoking. Add onions, whole jalapeños, poblanos, and garlic. Sauté well. Add potatoes, chicken stock, parsley, and thyme. Bring to a boil. Simmer for 30 minutes.

In a food processor or blender, purée soup until smooth. Season to taste with salt, pepper, and cayenne. Chill completely. When cold, gently fold in cream. Garnish with herbed croutons, crème fraîche, or marinated vegetables.

⌂ Inn of the Anasazi
Santa Fe, New Mexico

The Inn of the Anasazi celebrates the enduring and creative spirit of the early Native Americans known as the Anasazi. The inn's restaurant features culinary legacies of the Southwest including foods of the earth from Native Americans; foods of the soul from Northern New Mexico; and foods of substance favored by the American cowboy. Exciting dishes are made with combinations of natural ingredients from locally-grown organic produce.

A small, private wine cellar seats up to 12 guests, maintains an inventory of premier wines, and stores private stock for patrons. The cocktail lounge is a perfect place to renew ones spirit with friends and fellow travelers.

⬚ *Princely Peach Soup*

Soup for breakfast? Yes! Princely Peach Soup is a welcome morning treat at The King's Cottage during the hot summer months. Innkeepers, Karen and Jim Owens, serve a memorable feast. The imaginative gourmet menu includes freshly-brewed coffee, fine teas, fresh-squeezed juices, homemade breads, and a special dish such as Peaches & Cream French Toast and Cranberry Poached Apples.

Makes 4 refreshing servings.

6 large, very ripe peaches
4 tablespoons sour cream
1/4 cup orange juice
1/8 cup lemon juice
1/4 cup powdered sugar
1/8 teaspoon cinnamon

Nutmeg & ground cloves to taste
Whipped cream (or heavy cream)
4 sprigs fresh mint

Peel, pit, and dice the peaches. In food processor or blender, purée the peaches until they are of a smooth consistency. Add sour cream, orange, and lemon juices, and powdered sugar. Mix until well blended. Add spices and mix again. Refrigerate for at least 4 hours and serve cold.

Garnish each serving with a dollop of whipped cream and a sprig of mint. Or pour heavy cream in the middle of soup and use a toothpick to make a star design.

↻ *The King's Cottage*
Lancaster, Pennsylvania

In 1995, The King's Cottage bed & breakfast was named to the American Historic Inn's "Top 10 List." The 1912 Spanish-style mansion was honored for excellence in hospitality, elegance, service, location, and charm. The inn's located just minutes from the Pennsylvania Amish countryside. According to the owners, "It's perfect for a romantic getaway. Honeymooners and second honeymooners love the privacy of the Carriage House." During they're stay, guests are pampered with an afternoon tea and treated to complimentary cordials by the fire in the evening.

⎕ *Two Melon Soup*

Chilled fruit soups are a refreshing breakfast item on the menu at The King's Cottage. The inn is located just outside the city limits of Lancaster, Pennsylvania, the one time (1777) capitol of the United States.

Innkeepers, Jim and Karen Owens, serve breakfast at a common table in the formal dining room. The eye-opening meal overflows with freshly made gourmet dishes like Strawberry Poached Pears drizzled with melted chocolate and topped with whipped cream or an upscale oatmeal souffle made with cream cheese, brown sugar, cinnamon, raisins, walnuts, and maple syrup. Breakfasts are served with down-to-earth Lancaster County bacon.

Serves 6.

1 ripe cantaloupe, seeded &
 diced
2 tablespoons fresh lemon
 juice
1 honeydew melon, same size
 as cantaloupe, seeded &
 diced

2 tablespoons fresh lime juice
1-1/2 teaspoons minced fresh
 mint, or to taste
Mint sprigs for garnish

In a blender, purée cantaloupe with lemon juice until smooth. Transfer to a container and refrigerate, covered, for at least 3 hours. Rinse out blender. Purée honeydew melon with lime juice and mint until smooth. Transfer second purée to another container and refrigerate, covered, for at least 3 hours.

At serving time, transfer purées to separate containers with pouring spouts. With one container in each hand, simultaneously pour equal amounts of the purées into individual serving bowls. The purées will stay separated, with the cantaloupe on one side and the honeydew on the other, even when carried to the table and while being eaten. Garnish each dish with a sprig of mint.

⎕ *Mango Melon Soup*

The Two Sisters Inn doesn't serve lunch or dinner, but they do shine at breakfast. This recipe is a refreshing soup served as part of their three-course gourmet wake-up call.

Makes 6 servings.

1 small melon, peeled & cubed
1 ripe banana, peeled
1 mango, peeled & cubed, divided
1 tablespoon lemon juice

1 tablespoon honey
Dash vanilla
6 mint leaves & 6 raspberries for garnish

Place melon cubes in blender and process until smooth. Add banana, 1/4 cup of the mango cubes, lemon juice, honey, and dash of vanilla. Blend until smooth. Chill mixture for several hours or overnight. Chill remaining mango cubes separately.

When ready to serve, divide mango cubes among 6 parfait cups. Stir chilled soup and pour equally over the fruit. Garnish with raspberries and mint leaves.

⌂ Two Sisters Inn
Manitou Springs, Colorado

Nestled at the base of Pikes Peak, the two-story Two Sisters Inn was built in 1919 by two sisters who used it as a boarding house. The rose-colored Victorian bungalow has been transformed into four bedrooms with original bedsteads, hand-pressed linens, and plenty of fresh flowers. The cozy honeymoon cottage in the back garden contains a white wicker bedroom set with a feather bed, romantic gas log fireplace, and a skylight to reflect the rich Colorado sky.

The inn is quiet, convenient, and situated a short block from the center of town. Nearby diversions include mineral springs, art galleries, shops, and restaurants.

Chilled Fruit Soups

☐ Pineapple Mint Energy Bisque

In keeping with the heightened demand for a healthy, active life-style, restaurants at the Buena Vista Palace feature a number of delicious "Spa Cuisine" offerings such as this Pineapple Mint Energy Bisque.

Makes 4 servings.

1 chilled pineapple, cleaned, 1/2 of the shell reserved	1 teaspoon brewers yeast
8 sprigs mint	1 mint tip for garnish
2 ounces soft tofu	6 tablespoons chilled, diced pineapple for garnish
1/4 cup nonfat yogurt	

Juice whole pineapple, except for reserve, in a juice machine, to produce approximately 20 ounces of liquid. Juice mint. Pour pineapple and mint juices into a blender with tofu, yogurt, and brewers yeast. Blend mixture well. Pour into the 1/2 pineapple shell. Garnish bisque with diced pineapple and mint.

♙ Buena Vista Palace Spa & Resort
Lake Buena Vista, Florida

A stay at the 1,014-room Buena Vista Palace Resort & Spa at Walt Disney World Village is a dream vacation for both parents and kids. After a fun-filled day with Mickey Mouse and his friends, parents can return to the resort's European-style spa and indulge in a soothing massage or a refreshing herbal wrap. Children may attend supervised evening fun at the Kid's Stuff/Kid's Night Out activity program.

This all-in-one resort contains a modern fitness center, three swimming pools, tennis courts, a marina with boat rentals, a game arcade, children's playground, and access to five Walt Disney championship golf courses.

On-site eateries include the award-winning Arthur's 27 restaurant with panoramic views from its 27th-floor location and the Australian-themed Outback Restaurant. Children of all ages love dining with Minnie Mouse, Pluto, and Goofy on Sunday morning at the lakeside Watercress Cafe and Bakery.

⬚ Chilled Pear and Beetroot Soup Garnished with Ginger and Cinnamon Croutons

Taste-tempting creations are prepared and presented with panache by talented chefs in Nisbet's tropical restaurant, Coconuts.

Serves 10.

2 medium fresh beetroot
 (about 12 ounces each)
Poaching liquid for pears:
 3 quarts water
 1 cup white wine
 3/4 cups white sugar
 1 large vanilla bean, cut &
  scraped
 2 large cinnamon sticks
 1/2 cup fresh lime juice
 1/2 cup frozen orange juice
  concentrate

4 pounds Bosc pears
2 cups fresh milk
2 cups heavy cream
1/2 cup Grand Marnier (an
 orange-flavored cognac)
For croutons:
 1/4 cup unsalted butter
 1 teaspoon finely chopped
  fresh ginger
 5 slices toast bread, cubed
 1 teaspoon cinnamon

Steam whole, washed beetroot until cooked and place in cold water. Rub off peel with a towel. In a stockpot, bring poaching liquid ingredients to a boil. Poach peeled and cored pears for 20 minutes or until soft. Remove cinnamon sticks. Slice beets and add to pears and poaching liquid. Purée in a juice blender until smooth. Add fresh milk, heavy cream, and Grand Marnier. Chill in refrigerator. To prepare croutons, heat butter and ginger in a frying pan. Add bread crumbs and toss until golden brown. Add ground cinnamon. Sprinkle croutons on soup just before serving.

↻ Nisbet Plantation Beach Club
Nevis, West Indies

In a setting of coconut palms, a white coral sand beach, and cooling offshore breezes, the gracious Nesbit Plantation Beach Club provides a tropical paradise where guests may unwind and relax, participate in stimulating outdoor activities, and enjoy fine dining experiences.

After a day of swimming, sailing, sport fishing, snorkeling, scuba diving, horseback riding, golf, and tennis, the Nesbit Plantation Beach Club's restaurant offers a diverse bounty of impressive taste-tempting creations.

Chilled Fruit Soups

⎕ Apple Soup with Roquefort Croutons

This warm sweet soup from The Inn at Cedar Falls is just right for a chilly fall evening.

Serves 8.

6 tablespoons butter
1-1/4 pounds (about 3 large) Red Delicious apples, peeled, cored, & sliced
1-1/4 pounds (about 3 large) Granny Smith apples, peeled, cored, & sliced
1 cup chopped onion
2 cloves garlic, minced
5 cups chicken broth
1-1/2 cups heavy cream
Salt & pepper to taste
1 *each* Red Delicious & Granny Smith apple, cored (leave peel on) for garnish
2 tablespoons fresh lemon juice
2 tablespoons chopped chives
Roquefort Croutons (recipe follows)

Melt 4 tablespoons of the butter in a large saucepan. Add the 1-1/4 pounds Red Delicious and Granny Smith apples, onion, and garlic. Cook for 5 minutes. Add chicken broth and simmer until apples are very tender, about 25 minutes. Purée mixture in food processor. Return purée to pan. Stir in cream and simmer. Season to taste with salt and pepper.

To prepare garnish, cut Red Delicious apple into 16 thin slices and Granny Smith apple into 8 slices. Mix with lemon juice. Melt remaining 2 tablespoons butter in skillet. Add apples and sauté until golden brown.

To serve, ladle soup into bowls. Top each bowl with 2 Red Delicious and 1 Granny Smith apple slices. Sprinkle with chopped chives. Serve with croutons.

Roquefort Croutons

1/4 cup olive oil
3 cloves garlic, minced
2 teaspoons fresh parsley
2 teaspoons fresh basil
1/2 cup Roquefort cheese
8 thick, cut on the diagonal, slices French bread
Salt & pepper

In a small bowl, combine oil, garlic, parsley, basil, and Roquefort. Mix well. Spread 1 side of bread with a generous amount of mixture. Sprinkle lightly with salt and pepper. Arrange French bread slices on a baking sheet. Bake at 350 degrees until golden, about 15 minutes.

Warm Fruit Soups

The Inn at Cedar Falls
Logan, Ohio

The Inn at Cedar Falls is comfortably rustic. Its surroundings peaceful and in tune with nature. The inn's 60-acre site is abundant with wildlife and near the rock formations, waterfalls, and caves of Hocking Hills State Park.

Guest rooms combine the charm of antique beds, private baths, and views of nearby meadows and woods. Guests may choose to stay in a room in the main house or in one of the inn's five renovated 19th century log cabins.

The heart of the inn, the kitchen, provides country gourmet fare based on seasonal foods. All the herbs and homegrown vegetables used in cooking are picked fresh from the surrounding gardens. Guests are delighted to discover their favorite recipes in *The Inn at Cedar Falls Cookbook.*

Warm Fruit Soups

☐ *Banana-Coconut-Chicken Soup*

Dining at The Golden Lemon is a moveable feast. Most guests have breakfast in bed. Lunch is usually served on the great house gallery. Dinner can be savored on the gallery, in the garden, poolside, or in the magnificent dining room, which is one of the most photographed rooms on St. Kitts.

Makes 6 servings.

2 medium onions, peeled & chopped	1 cup evaporated milk
4 teaspoons butter	1 cup chicken stock
1-1/3 cups milk	1/2 cup grated coconut
	1 banana, fairly ripe

Sauté onions in butter until golden brown. Add both milks and chicken stock. Bring to a boil, then simmer for 5 minutes. Put in a blender with coconut and banana. Blend until smooth. Transfer to saucepan and return to a boil. Simmer for 5 minutes.

⌘ The Golden Lemon Inn and Villas
Dieppe Bay, St. Kitts, West Indies

For several decades, The Golden Lemon Inn has provided friendly hospitality and delicious culinary delights. The story of the property's rehabilitation and name deserves to be told.

The main house was built in 1615 and was in ramshackle condition when Arthur Leaman bought it in the early 1960s. A decorating editor at *House and Garden* magazine, Leaman had a new roof installed and modernized the building by adding electricity and running water. He saw the potential when no one else did. When friends referred to the place as "a lemon," he quickly remarked, "It had better be a golden one!" Thus, the name.

The great house and annex has eight guest rooms. Fifteen condominiums, each with private plunge pools, on a Hawaiian-style black sand beach. All units are individually furnished with local antiques, island art, and fresh flowers.

Warm Fruit Soups

Contributor's Directory

Page numbers in **bold** include descriptive information.

66 **The Adolphus.** 1321 Commerce, Dallas, TX 75202. (214) 742-8200.

103 **Ash, Chef John.** c/o Fetzer Valley Oaks. P.O. Box 611, Hopland, CA 95449. (707) 744-1250.

122 **Bellevue Hotel.** Broad & Walnut Streets, Philadelphia, PA 19102. (215) 893-1776.

147 **Black Cat Guest Ranch.** Box 6267, Hinton AB, Canada T7V 1X6. (780) 865-3084.

52 **Blueberry Hills Inn.** Goshen, VT 05733. (802) 247-6735.

64 **Boston Park Plaza Hotel.** 64 Arlington Street at Park Plaza, Boston, MA 02116-3912. (800) 225-2008.

176 **Buena Vista Palace Spa & Resort.** 1900 Buena Vista Drive, Lake Buena Vista, FL 32830. (800) 327-2990.

29 **Butterfield Bed & Breakfast.** P.O. Box 1115, 2284 Sunset Drive, Julian, CA 90236. (760) 765-2179.

69 **Cafe Parizäde.** 2300 West Main Street, Durham, NC 27701. (919)286-9712.

170 **Caffrey, Mavis.** c/o Gold Coast Press. 4360 East Main Street, Suite 129, Ventura, CA 93003. (805) 639-3976.

74 **Calla's Cooking School.** 8675 East Mud Lake Road, Baldwinsville, NY 13027.

135, 166 **Camelback Inn Resort.** Golf Club & Spa. 5402 East Lincoln Drive, Scottsdale, AZ 85253. (800) 24-CAMEL.

104 **Carter, Bob.** c/o Gold Coast Press, 4360 East Main Street, Suite 129, Ventura, CA 93003. (805) 639-3976.

101 **Casa Larga Vineyards.** 2287 Turk Hill Road, Fairport, NY 14450. (716) 223-4210.

57 **Cataloochee Ranch.** 119 Ranch Drive, Maggie Valley, NC 28751. (828) 926-1401.

152 **Cathcart, Maxine.** c/o The Valley Messenger. 35242 Yucaipa Boulevard, Suite 3, Yucaipa, CA 92399. (909) 790-9470.

118 **Chandler's Crabhouse and Fresh Fish Market.** 901 Fairview Avenue North, Seattle, WA 98109. (206) 223-CRAB.

113 **Chatham Bars Inn.** Shore Road, Chatham, MA 02633. (508) 945-0096. (800) 527-4884.

165 **Christian's Restaurant.** Tutwiler Hotel. 2021 Park Place North, Birmingham, AL 35203.

40, **132** **Christopher Ranch.** 305 Bloomfield Avenue, Gilroy, CA 95020. (408) 847-1100.

80 **Cinnamon Hearts.** P.O. Box 578340, Modesto, CA 95357. (209) 572-0769.

120, 168   **The Colony Beach & Tennis Resort.** 1620 Gulf of Mexico Drive, Longboat Key, FL 34228-3499. (941) 383-6464, (800) 4-COLONY.

114   **Crackers Seafood Restaurant at Church Street Station.** 129 West Church Street, Orlando, FL 32801. (407) 422-2434.

30, 65   **The Culinary Sleuth.** P.O. Box 194, Bryn Mawr, PA 19010.

68   **Deer Path Inn.** 255 East Illinois Road, Lake Forest, IL 60045. (800) 788-9480.

44, 45   **Deer Valley Resort.** P.O. Box 1525, Park City, UT 84060.

154   **Farmers Market.** 6333 West 3rd Street, Los Angeles, CA 90036. (323) 931-3773.

160   **The Fearrington Market Cafe.** 2000 Fearrington Village Center, Pittsboro, NC 27312. (919) 542-5505.

145   **Filomena's.** 2810 South Harbor Boulevard, Oxnard, CA 93035. (805) 984-6388.

56, 127   **Four Seasons Resort.** P.O. Box 565, Pinney's Beach, Charlestown, Nevis, West Indies. (809) 469-1111.

35, 157   **Fullers.** Seattle Sheraton Hotel & Towers. 1400 Sixth Avenue, Seattle, WA 98101. (206) 389-5544 or (206) 621-9000

180   **The Golden Lemon Inn and Villas.** Dieppe Bay, St. Kitts, West Indies. (809) 465-7260.

50, 148   **The Governor's Inn.** 86 Main Street, Ludlow, VT 05149. (802) 228-8830 or (800) GOVERNOR.

81   **Granby House Bed and Breakfast.** 101 Granby Street, Toronto, Ontario, Canada, M5B 1H9. (416) 596-8703.

31, 34   **Grandview Lodge.** 466 Lickstone Road, Waynesville, NC 28786. (828) 456-5212.

63   **Great Taste of Pennsylvania Wine & Food Festival.** Split Rock Resort and Conference Center. Lake Harmony, PA 18624. (570) 722-9111 or (800) 255-ROCK.

117, 124   **The Grove Park Inn Resort.** 290 Macon Avenue, Asheville, NC 28804-3799. (800) 438-5800.

48   **Harrah's Casino.** 219 North Center Street, Reno, NV 89501. (775) 788-3028.

92   **Healthy Exchanges.** P.O. Box 124, DeWitt, IA 52742-0124. (319) 659-8234.

79, 138   **Hobbs, Gail.** c/o Gold Coast Press, 3100 Whisper Oaks Way, Bakersfield, CA 93311. (661) 665-2132.

139   **The Hollywood Chef, Vern Langrasse.** 1536 North Orange Grove Avenue, Hollywood, CA 90046.

167 **Hyatt Regency Scottsdale Resort at Gainey Ranch.** 7500 East Doubletree Ranch Road, Scottsdale, AZ 85258. (480) 991-3388.

178, 179 **The Inn at Cedar Falls.** 21190 State Route 374, Logan, OH 43138. (740) 385-7489.

89, 172 **Inn of the Anasazi.** 113 Washington Avenue, Santa Fe, NM 87501. (505) 988-3030 or (800) 688-8100.

47 **The Jefferson.** 1200 Sixteenth Street NW, Washington, D.C. 20036. (202) 347-2200.

51, 53 **The Jefferson Hotel.** 101 West Franklin Street, Richmond, VA 23220. (804) 788-8000.

125 **Jekyll Island Club Hotel.** 371 Riverview Drive, Jekyll Island, GA 31520. (912) 635-2600.

41, 134 **Jumpin' Jacks–Cafe on the Water.** 100 Willow Creek Drive, Kohler, WI 53044. (920) 457-4445.

32 **Kilauea Lodge.** P.O. Box 116, Volcano Village, HI 96785. (808) 967-7366.

173, 174 **The King's Cottage.** 1049 East King Street, Lancaster, PA 17602. (717) 397-1017.

43 **L'Auberge Del Mar Resort & Spa.** P.O. Box 2889, 1540 Camino Del Mar at 15th Street, Del Mar, CA 92014. (800) 553-1336.

97 **L'Auberge Provencale.** P.O. Box 190, White Post, VA 22663. (540) 837-1375 or (800) 638-1702.

115 **Loews Santa Monica Beach Hotel.** 1700 Ocean Avenue, Santa Monica, CA 90401. (800) 23-LOEWS.

59 **Loews Ventana Canyon Resort.** 7000 North Resort Drive, Tucson, AZ 85750. (520) 299-2020.

169 **Magnolia Grill.** 1002 Ninth Street, Durham, NC 27705. (919) 286-3609.

46, 171 **The Mark.** Madison Avenue at East 77th Street, New York, NY 10021. (212) 744-4300 or (800) THE-MARK.

93 **Marriott's Bay Point Resort.** 4200 Marriott Drive, Panama City Beach, FL 32408. (850) 236-6000.

88 **Matteo, Chef Mike, Chef Mike's Catering.** 87 Walzer Road, Rochester, NY 14622.

26 **Maxwell's Restaurant & Lounge.** P.O. Box 946, 4207 East Clay Street, Vicksburg, MS 39180. (601) 636-1344.

150, 151 **Mission Inn.** 3649 Mission Inn Avenue, Riverside, CA 92501. (909) 784-0300.

55, 91 **Mohonk Mountain House.** 1000 Mountain Rest Road. Lake Mohonk, New Paltz, NY 12561. (845) 255-1000 or (800) 772-6646.

61 **Montpelier Plantation Inn.** P.O. Box 474, Nevis, West Indies. (809) 469-3462.

Contributor's Directory

126	**Mount Nevis Hotel & Beach Club.** P.O. Box 494, Nevis, West Indies. (800) 75-NEVIS.
177	**Nisbet Plantation Beach Club.** St. James Parish, Nevis, West Indies. (809) 469-9325.
28	**Nona's Courtyard Café.** 67 South California Street, Ventura, CA 93001. (805) 641-2783.
77	**Ojai Valley Inn.** 905 Country Club Road, Ojai, CA 93023. (805) 646-5511 or (800) 422-OJAI.
90	**Omni Netherland Plaza.** 35 West Fifth Street, Cincinnati, OH 45202. (513) 421-9100 or (800) THE-OMNI.
37, 42	**The Orchid at Mauna Lani.** One North Kaniku Drive, Kohala Coast, HI 96743. (808) 885-2000.
73	**Orinda Bed & Breakfast.** Box 4451, 461 Valverde, Taos, NM 87581. (505) 758-8581 or (800) 847-1837.
108	**Ottley's Plantation Inn.** P.O. Box 345, Basseterre, St. Kitts, West Indies. (809) 465-7234 or (800) 772-3039.
105	**Oualie Beach Hotel.** Oualie Bay, Jones Estate, Nevis, West Indies. (809) 469-9735.
58, 94	**The Peabody Orlando.** 9801 International Drive, Orlando, FL 32819. (407) 352-4000 or (800) PEABODY.
123	**The Pfister Hotel.** 424 East Wisconsin Avenue, Milwaukee, WI 53202. (414) 273-8222 or (800) 558-8222.
95, 162	**Pikes Peak Highland Games and Celtic Festival.** 529 Yellowstone Road, Colorado Springs, CO 80910.
140	**The Pontchartrain.** 2301 St. Charles Avenue, New Orleans, LA 70140. (504) 524-0581 or (800) 777-6193.
38	**Queen Mary.** 1126 Queens Highway, Long Beach, CA 90802-6390. (562) 435-3511.
33, 109 126	**Rabbit Hill Inn.** Lower Waterford, VT 05848. (802) 748-5168.
116	**Radisson Valley Center Hotel.** 15433 Ventura Boulevard, Sherman Oaks, CA 91403. (818) 981-5400.
62	**Rawlins Plantation Hotel & Restaurant.** Box 340, St. Kitts, West Indies. (809) 465-6221.
143	**Ristorante Villa Portofino.** 101 Crescent Avenue, Santa Catalina Island, CA. (310) 510-0555.
39	**The Rendezvous Inn & Restaurant.** 647 North Main Street, Fort Bragg, CA 95437. (800) 491-8142.
121	**Robin's Restaurant.** 4095 Burton Drive, Cambria, CA 93428. (805) 927-5007.
153	**St. Maarten.** 675 Third Avenue, New York, NY. 10017. (800) ST-MAARTEN.

161	**Sam Choy's Restaurants.** 73-5576 Kauhola Street, Kailua-Kona, HI 96740. (808) 326-1545.
96, 107	**Sandy Creek Manor House.** 1960 Redman Road, Hamlin, NY 14464. (716) 964-7528.
87	**Sanford Winery & Ranch.** 7250 Santa Rosa Road, Buellton, CA 93427. (805) 688-3300.
106	**Sheraton Moana Surfrider.** 2365 Kalakaua Avenue, Honolulu, HI 96815. (808) 922-3111 or (800) STAY-ITT.
133	**Silver Dollar City.** H.C.R. 1, Box 791, Branson, MO 65616-9602. (800) 952-6626.
144	**Sing & Cook Italian.** P.O. Box 91725, Santa Barbara, CA 93190-1725.
159	**Solar Cook-off.** Plumas County Visitors Bureau, P.O. Box 4120, Quincy, CA 95971. (530) 283-6345 or (800) 326-2247.
78, 86	**Sundance Resort.** Rural Route 3, Box A-1, Sundance, UT 84604. (801) 225-4107 or (800) 892-1600.
36	**The Sutton Place Hotel.** 21 East Bellevue Place, Chicago, IL 60611. (312) 266-2100 or (800) 606-8188.
67	**The Sutton Place Hotel.** 845 Burrard Street, Vancouver, BC V6Z 2K6. (604) 682-5511 or (800) 961-7555.
146	**Sylvia's Authentic Italian Restaurant & Class Act Dinner Theater.** 5115 Northeast Sandy Boulevard, Portland, OR 97213. (503) 288-6828.
75	**Texas Barbeque.** Pig Out Publications. 4245 Walnut Street, Kansas City, MO 64111. (800) 877-3119.
155	**Turnberry Isle Resort & Club.** 19355 Turnberry Way, Aventura, FL 33180-2401. (305) 935-3000.
175	**Two Sisters Inn.** Ten Otoe Place, Manitou Springs, CO 80829. (719) 685-9684 or (800) 2-SIS-INN.
131	**Union Station Hotel.** 1001 Broadway, Nashville, TN 37203. (615) 726-1001 or (800) 331-2123.
85	**Walnut Hills Restaurant.** 1214 Adams Street, Vicksburg, MS 39180. (601) 638-4910.
158	**Wasserman, Debra.** c/o Vegetarian Resource Group. P.O. Box 1463, Baltimore, MD 21203. (410) 366-VEGE.
119	**The Westin St. Francis.** Union Square, 335 Powell Street, San Francisco, CA 94102. (415) 397-7000.
49	**Weir, Joanne.** 2107 Pine Street, San Francisco, CA 94115. (415) 776-4200.
149	**Wigwam Resort.** 300 Indian School Road, Litchfield, Park, AZ 85340. (623) 935-3811 or (800) 327-0396.

Contributor's Directory

Recipe Index

Recipe Index

Recipe Notes

Recipe Notes

Recipe Notes

Recipe Notes